THE BIG BOOK OF GOSPEL SONGS

ISBN 0-634-01711-X

HAL•LEONARD®
CORPORATION
7777 W. BLUEMOUND RD. P.O. BOX 13819 MILWAUKEE, WI 53213

For all works contained herein:
Unauthorized copying, arranging, adapting, recording or public performance is an infringement of copyright.
Infringers are liable under the law.

Visit Hal Leonard Online at
www.halleonard.com

CONTENTS

- 4 Amazing Grace
- 7 Are You Walkin' and A-Talkin' for the Lord
- 10 Are You Washed in the Blood?
- 12 At Calvary
- 14 Because He Lives
- 20 Blessed Assurance
- 17 The Blood Will Never Lose Its Power
- 22 Brighten the Corner Where You Are
- 24 Broken and Spilled Out
- 28 Calvary Covers It All
- 30 Church in the Wildwood
- 32 The Day He Wore My Crown
- 38 Does Jesus Care?
- 40 Down at the Cross (Glory to His Name)
- 42 The Eastern Gate
- 44 Footsteps of Jesus
- 46 Give Me That Old Time Religion
- 48 God Will Take Care of You
- 35 Goodby, World, Goodby
- 50 Hallelujah, We Shall Rise
- 52 He
- 58 He Keeps Me Singing
- 55 He Looked Beyond My Fault
- 60 He Touched Me
- 62 He's Got the Whole World in His Hands
- 68 His Eye Is on the Sparrow
- 70 His Name Is Wonderful
- 72 Holy Spirit, Thou Art Welcome
- 74 How Great Thou Art
- 65 How Long Has It Been
- 76 I Am Loved
- 80 I Am Not Ashamed
- 87 I Bowed on My Knees and Cried Holy
- 90 I Love to Tell the Story
- 94 I Saw the Light
- 100 I Stand Amazed in the Presence
- 97 I Will Serve Thee
- 102 I'd Rather Have Jesus
- 104 I'll Fly Away
- 106 I'm Standing on the Solid Rock
- 108 In the Garden
- 110 Jesus Paid It All
- 112 Just a Little Talk with Jesus
- 114 The King Is Coming
- 117 The King of Who I Am
- 120 Lamb of Glory
- 130 Life's Railway to Heaven
- 127 The Lighthouse
- 132 The Lily of the Valley
- 134 Little Is Much When God Is in It

136	The Longer I Serve Him
138	Love Lifted Me
140	The Love of God
142	Mansion Over the Hilltop
145	Midnight Cry
148	More Than Wonderful
152	My God Is Real (Yes, God Is Real)
154	My Tribute
158	A New Name in Glory
160	Oh, How I Love Jesus
162	The Old Rugged Cross
164	On Jordan's Stormy Banks
166	Peace in the Valley
168	Precious Lord, Take My Hand
170	Precious Memories
176	Put Your Hand in the Hand
173	Ready to Go Home
180	Rise Again
183	Rock of Ages
184	Room at the Cross for You
186	Shall We Gather at the River?
188	Since Jesus Came into My Heart
190	Soon and Very Soon
193	Stepping on the Clouds
196	Sweet Beulah Land
202	Sweet By and By
199	Sweet, Sweet Spirit
204	Tears Are a Language God Understands
210	There Is Power in the Blood
207	There's Something About That Name
212	Turn Your Radio On
218	The Unclouded Day
220	Upon This Rock
215	Victory in Jesus
228	Wayfaring Stranger
234	We Are So Blessed
238	We Shall Behold Him
242	We'll Understand It Better By and By
231	What a Beautiful Day (For the Lord to Come Again)
244	What a Day That Will Be
246	When I Can Read My Title Clear
248	When the Roll Is Called Up Yonder
254	When We All Get to Heaven
256	Why Me? (Why Me, Lord?)
251	Will the Circle Be Unbroken
258	Wings of a Dove
264	Without Him
266	The Wonder of It All
268	Written in Red
261	You Make It Rain for Me

AMAZING GRACE

Words by JOHN NEWTON
From *A Collection of Sacred Ballads*
Traditional American Melody
From Carrell and Clayton's *Virginia Harmony*
Arranged by EDWIN O. EXCELL

A-
maz - ing grace! how sweet the sound that
man - y dan - gers, toils and snares, I
when this flesh and heart shall fail and

saved a wretch like me! I once was
have al - rea - dy come. 'Tis grace hath
mor - tal life shall cease, I shall pos -

Copyright © 2001 by HAL LEONARD CORPORATION
International Copyright Secured All Rights Reserved

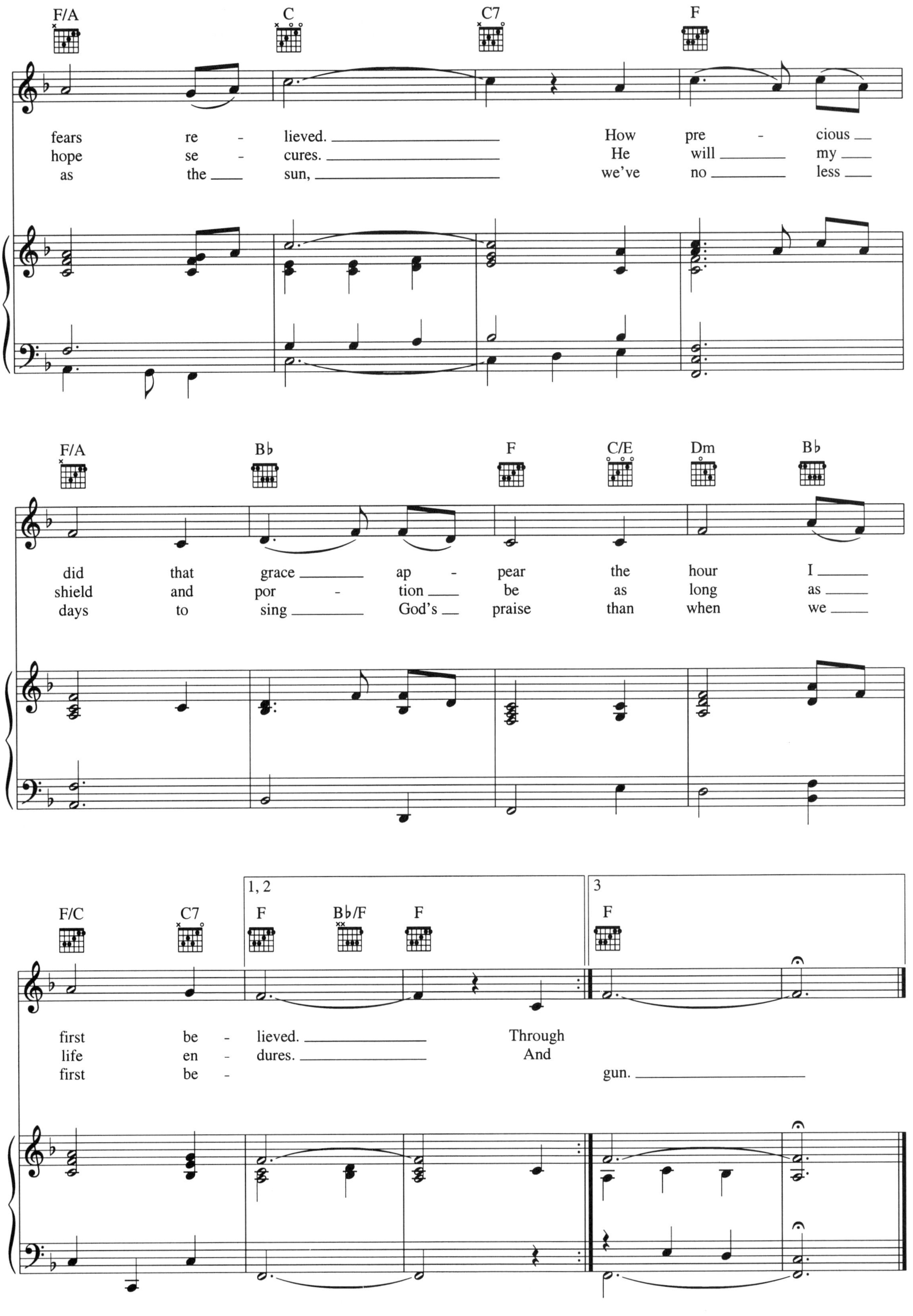
F/A
C
C7
F
fears re - lieved. How pre - cious
hope se - cures. He will my
as the sun, we've no less
F/A
B♭
F
C/E
Dm
B♭
did that grace ap - pear the hour I
shield and por - tion be as long as
days to sing God's praise than when we
F/C
C7
1, 2
F
B♭/F
F
3
F
first be - lieved. Through
life en - dures. And
first be - gun.

Are You Walkin' and A-Talkin' For The Lord

Words and Music by
HANK WILLIAMS

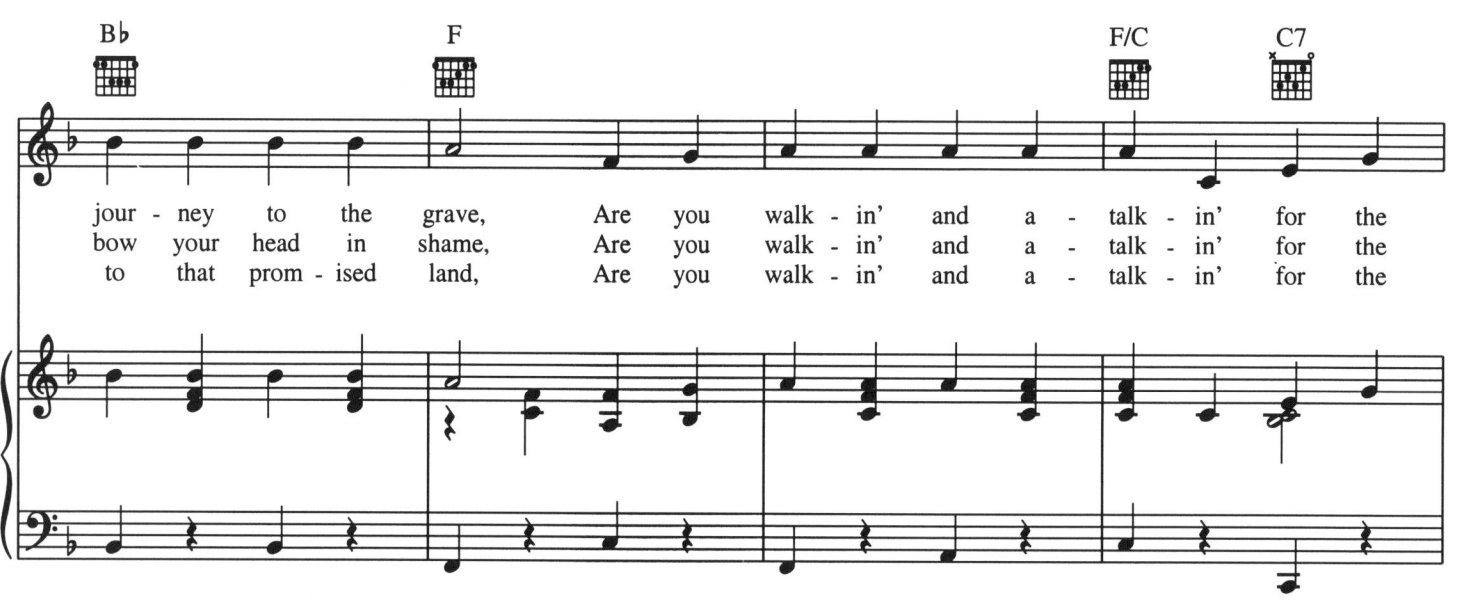

ARE YOU WASHED IN THE BLOOD?

Words and Music by
ELISHA A. HOFFMAN

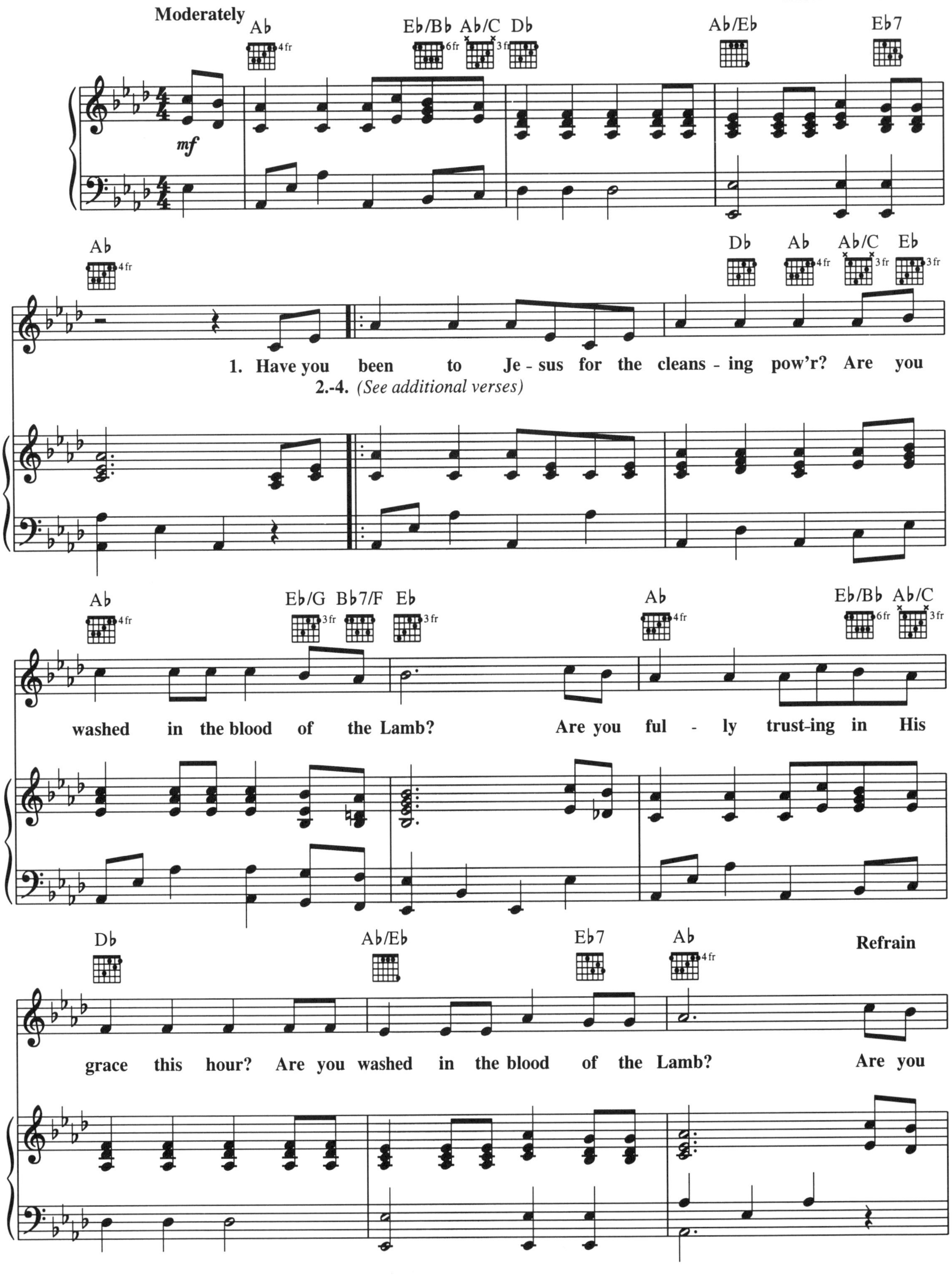

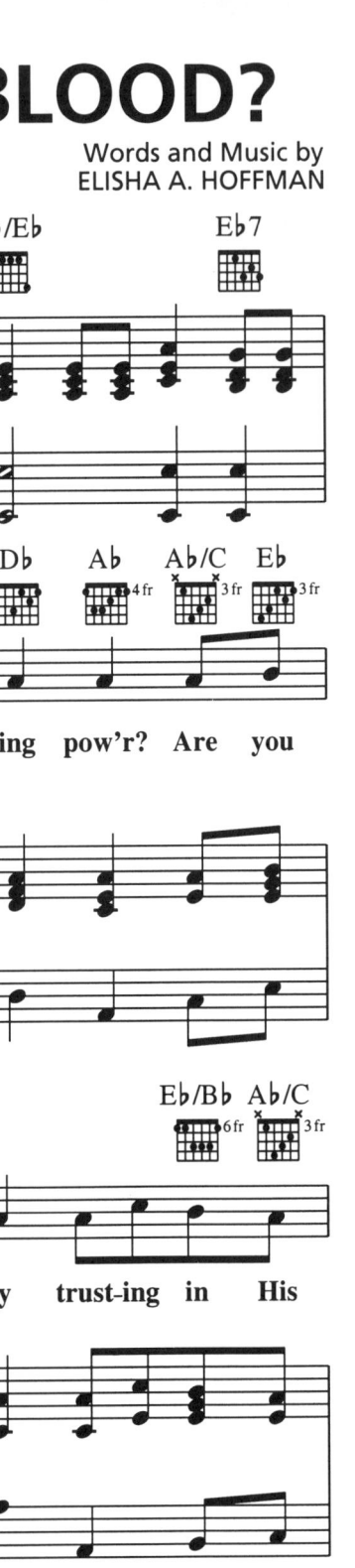

Additional Verses

2. Are you walking daily by the Savior's side?
   Are you washed in the blood of the Lamb?
   Do you rest each moment in the Crucified?
   Are you washed in the blood of the Lamb?
   Refrain

3. When the Bridegroom cometh will your robes be white?
   Are you washed in the blood of the Lamb?
   Will your soul be ready for the mansions bright,
   And be washed in the blood of the Lamb?
   Refrain

4. Lay aside the garments that are stained with sin,
   And be washed in the blood of the Lamb;
   There's a fountain flowing for the soul unclean,
   O be washed in the blood of the Lamb!
   Refrain

AT CALVARY

Words by WILLIAM R. NEWELL
Music by DANIEL B. TOWNER

Copyright © 1996 by HAL LEONARD CORPORATION
International Copyright Secured   All Rights Reserved

Additional Verses

2. By God's Word at last my sin I learned;
   Then I trembled at the law I'd spurned,
   Till my guilty soul imploring turned To Calvary.
   Refrain

3. Now I've giv'n to Jesus ev'rything,
   Now I gladly own Him as my King,
   Now my raptured soul can only sing Of Calvary.
   Refrain

4. Oh, the love that drew salvation's plan!
   Oh, the grace that bro't it down to man!
   Oh, the mighty gulf that God did span At Calvary.
   Refrain

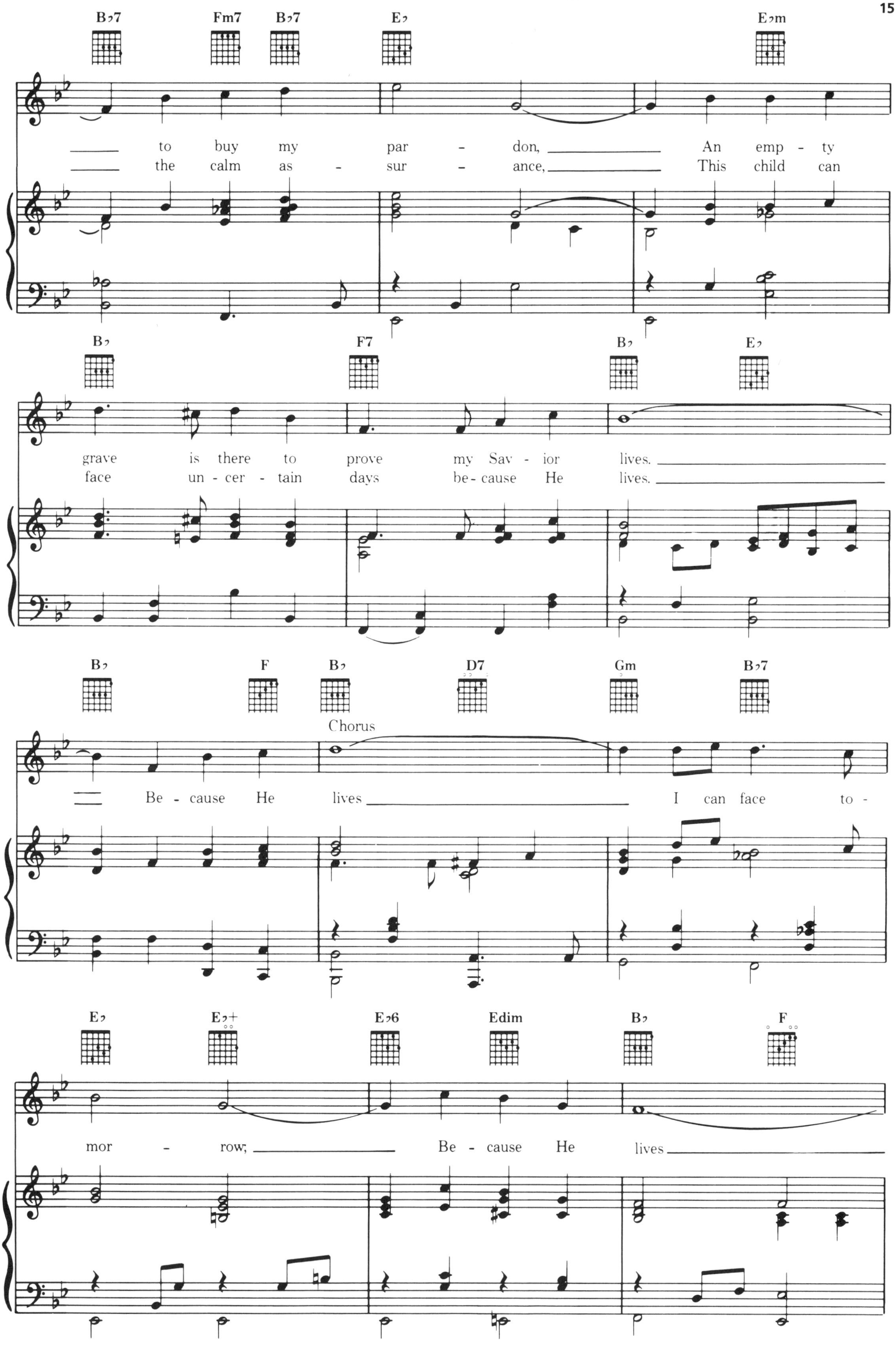

to buy my par - don, _____ An emp - ty
the calm as - sur - ance, _____ This child can

grave is there to prove my Sav - ior lives. _____
face un - cer - tain days be - cause He lives. _____

Chorus
___ Be - cause He lives _____ I can face to -

mor - row; _____ Be - cause He lives _____

3. And then one day I'll cross that river;
I'll fight life's final war with pain;
And then as death gives way to vict'ry,
I'll see the lights of glory and I'll know He reigns.

THE BLOOD WILL NEVER LOSE ITS POWER

Words and Music by
ANDRAÉ CROUCH

© Copyright 1966 (Renewed 1994) by MANNA MUSIC, INC., 35255 Brooten Road, Pacific City, OR 97135
All Rights Reserved Used by Permission

BLESSED ASSURANCE

Lyrics by FANNY J. CROSBY
Music by PHOEBE PALMER KNAPP

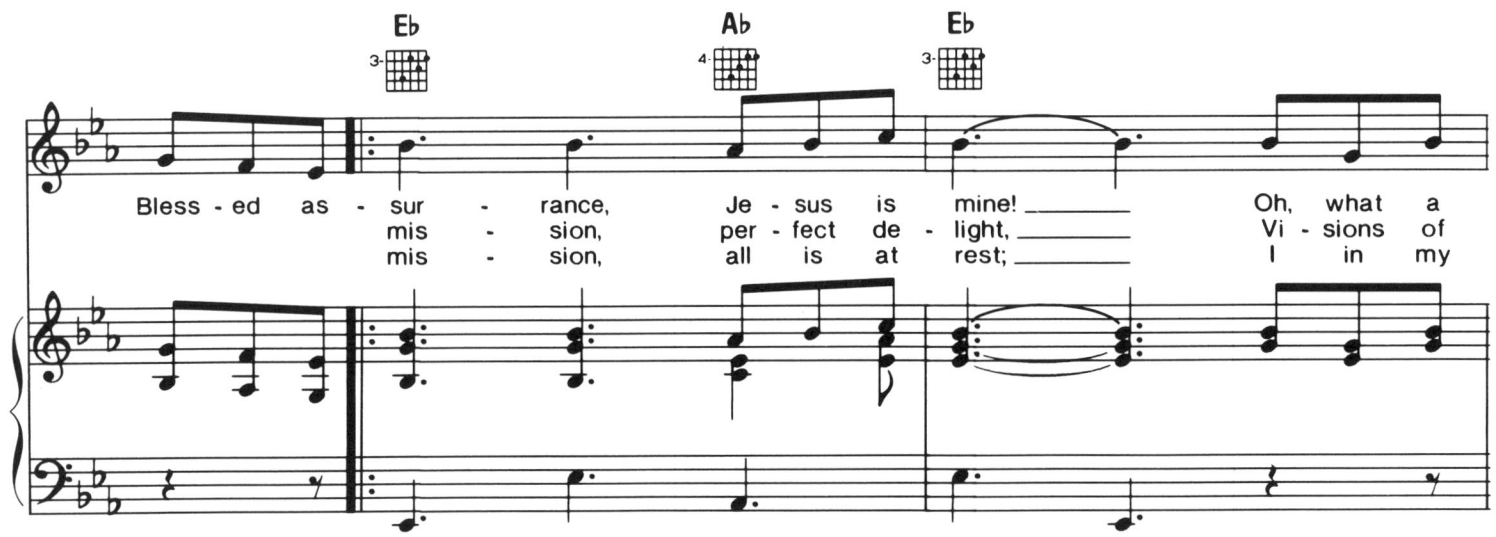

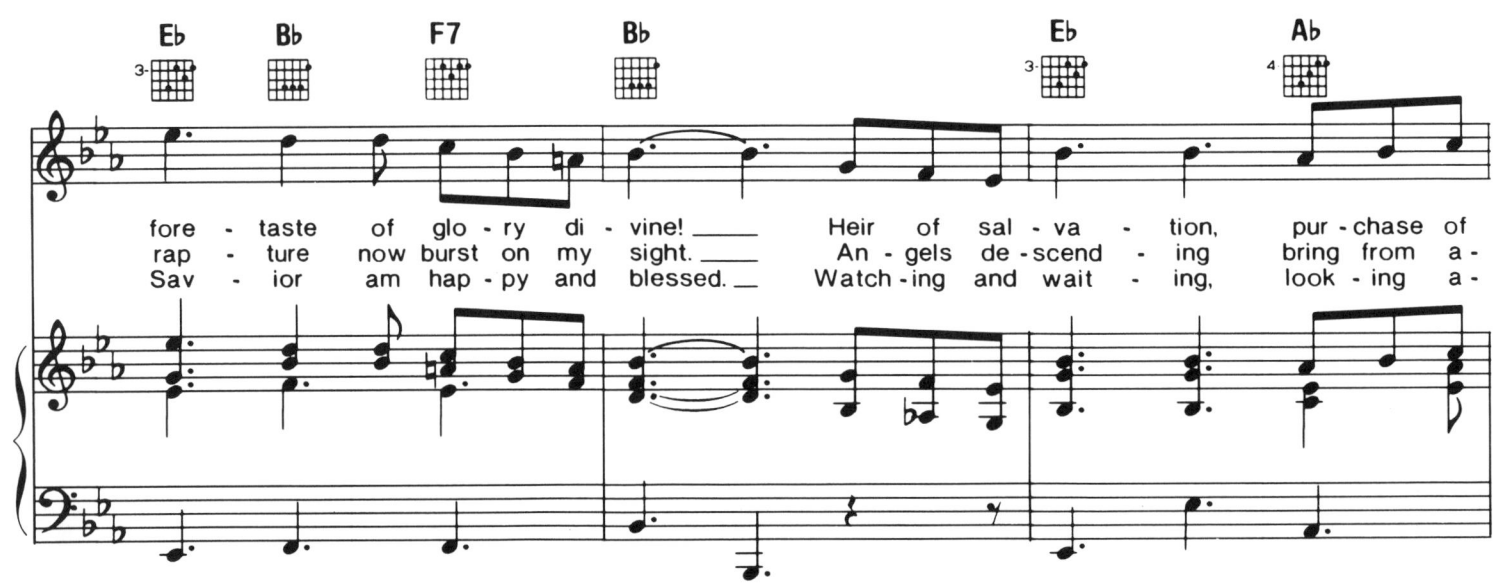

Copyright © 1983 by HAL LEONARD CORPORATION
International Copyright Secured All Rights Reserved

Brighten the Corner Where You Are

Words by INA DULEY OGDON
Music by CHARLES H. GABRIEL

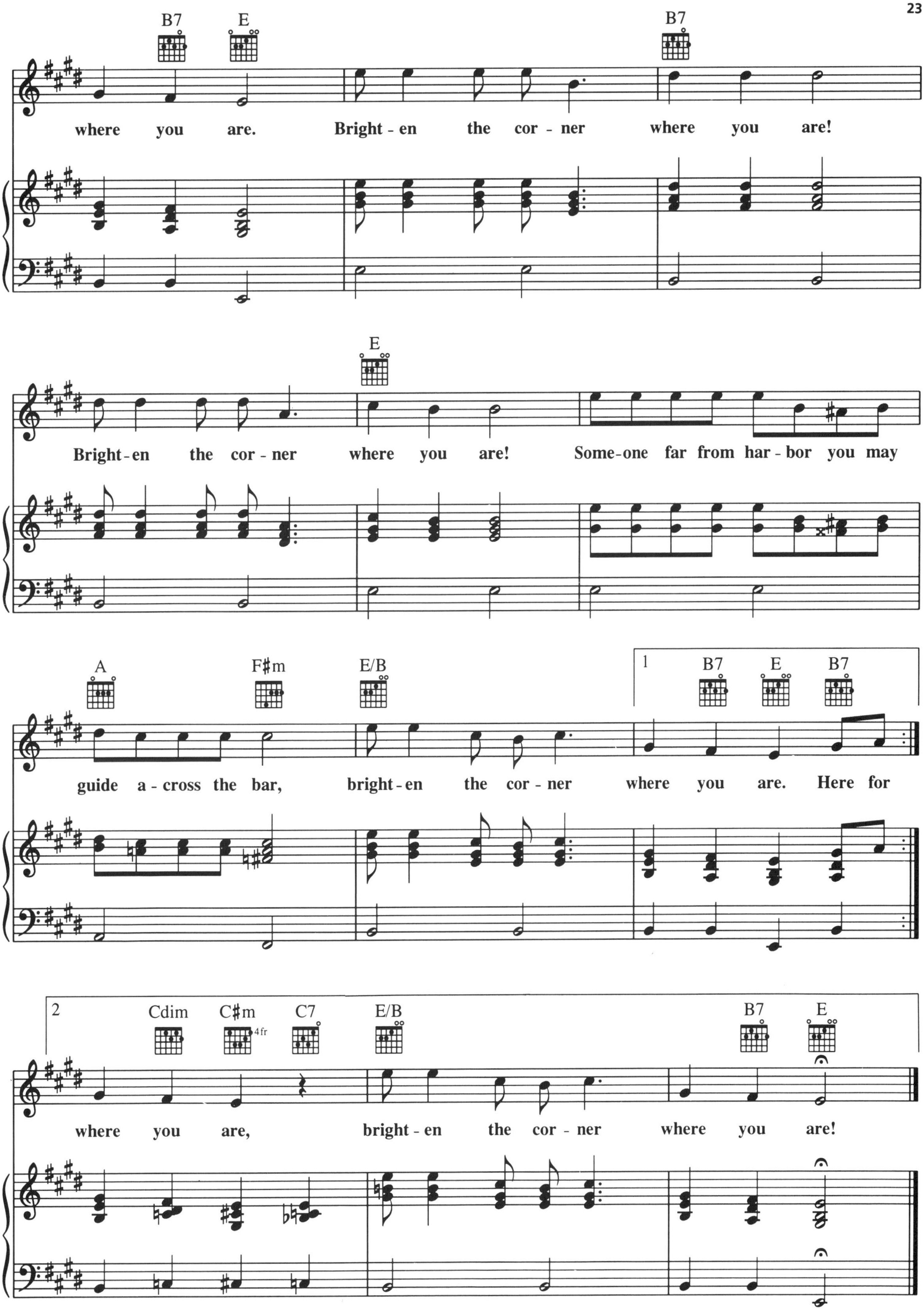
B7 E B7
where you are. Bright-en the cor-ner where you are!
E
Bright-en the cor-ner where you are! Some-one far from har-bor you may
A F♯m E/B
guide a-cross the bar, bright-en the cor-ner
1 B7 E B7
where you are. Here for
2 Cdim C♯m 4fr C7 E/B B7 E
where you are, bright-en the cor-ner where you are!

CALVARY COVERS IT ALL

Words and Music by
MRS. WALTER TAYLOR

Tenderly

Far dearer than all that the world can im-part was the mes-sage that came to my heart; _____ how that Je-sus a-lone for my sin did a-tone, and Cal-va-ry cov-ers it

stripes that He bore and the thorns that He wore told His mer-cy and love ev-er-more; _____ and my heart bowed in shame as I called on His name,

© 1931 (Renewed 1960) Word Music, Inc.
All Rights Reserved   Used by Permission

CHURCH IN THE WILDWOOD

Words and Music by
DR. WILLIAM S. PITTS

Copyright © 2001 by HAL LEONARD CORPORATION
International Copyright Secured All Rights Reserved

DOWN AT THE CROSS
(Glory to His Name)

Words by ELISHA A. HOFFMAN
Music by JOHN H. STOCKTON

FOOTSTEPS OF JESUS

Words by MARY B.C. SLADE
Music by ASA B. EVERETT

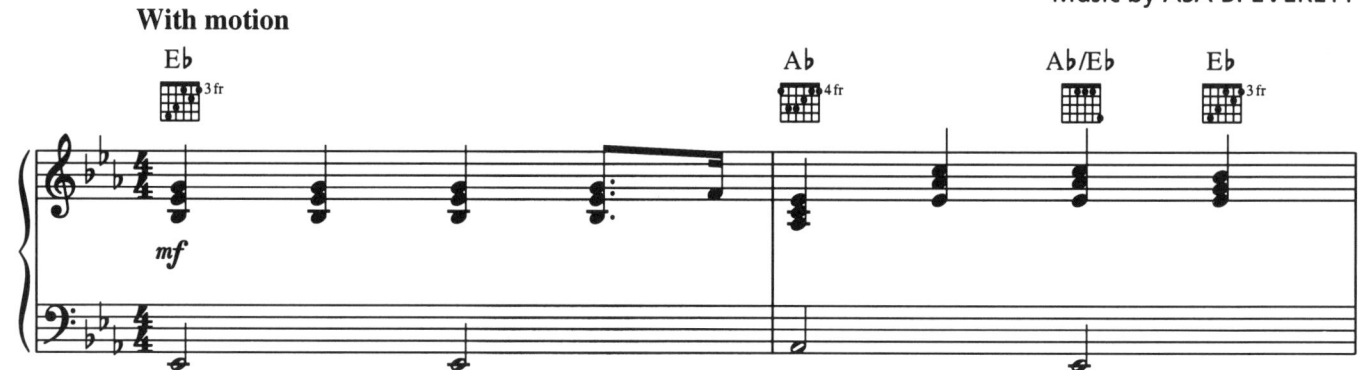
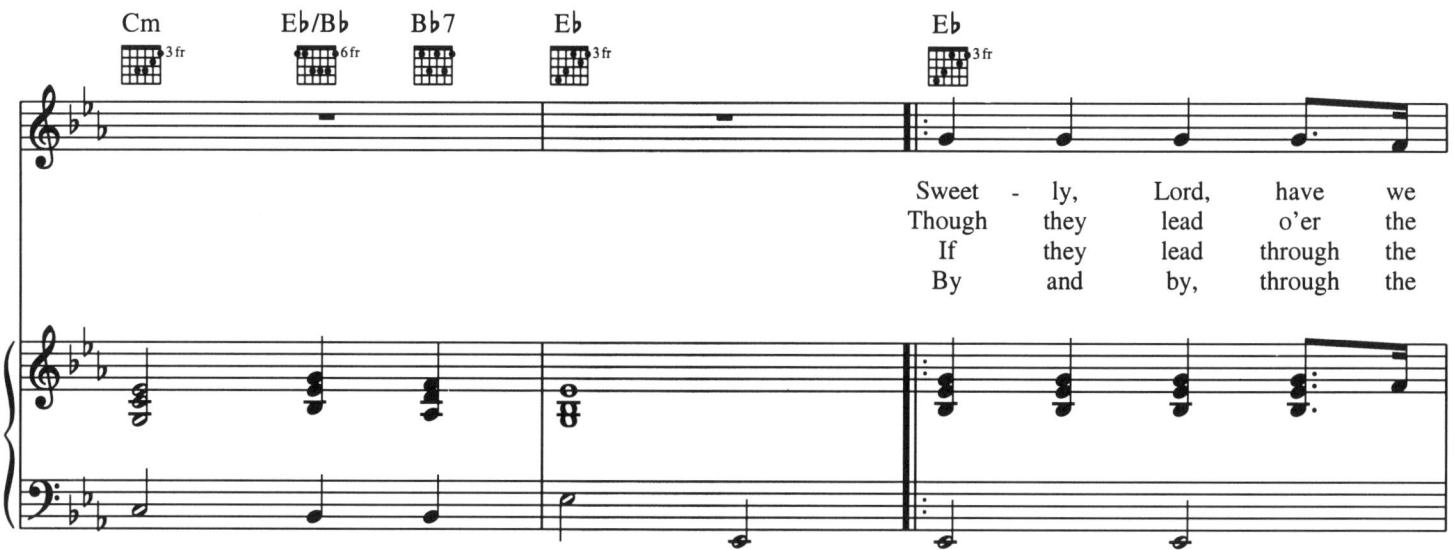
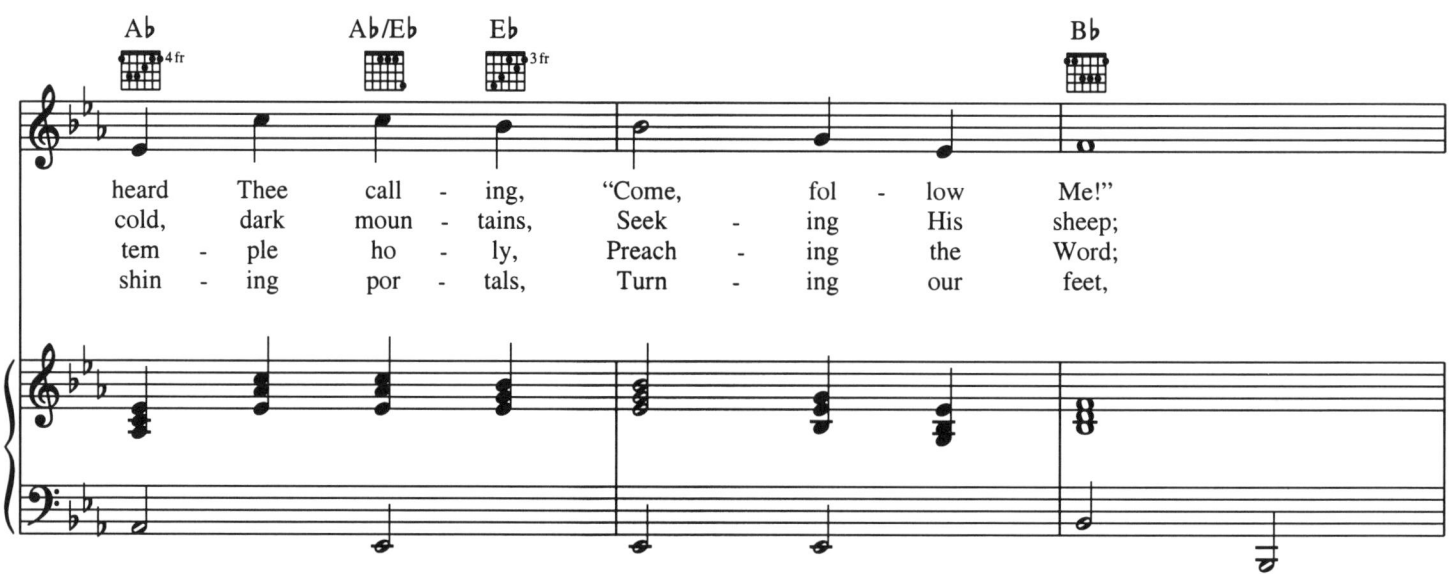

Sweet- ly, Lord, have we heard Thee call- ing, "Come, fol- low Me!"
Though they lead o'er the cold, dark moun- tains, Seek- ing His sheep;
If they lead through the tem- ple ho- ly, Preach- ing the Word;
By and by, through the shin- ing por- tals, Turn- ing our feet,

3. It was good for old Abe Lincoln;
   It was good for old Abe Lincoln.
   It was good for old Abe Lincoln,
   And it's good enough for me.

GOD WILL TAKE CARE OF YOU

Words by CIVILLA D. MARTIN
Music by W. STILLMAN MARTIN

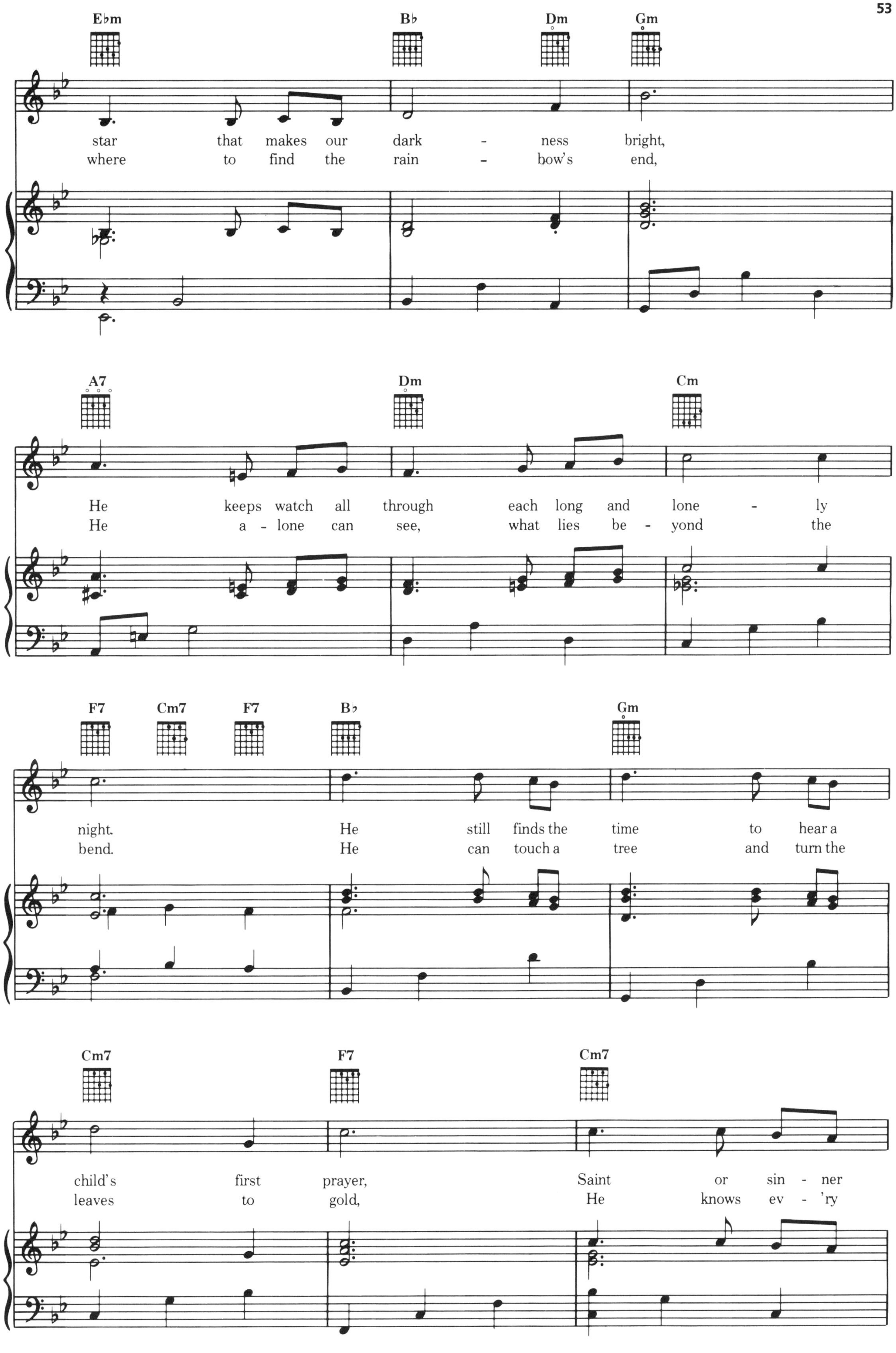
E♭m B♭ Dm Gm
star that makes our dark - ness bright,
where to find the rain - bow's end,
A7 Dm Cm
He keeps watch all through each long and lone - ly
He a - lone can see, what lies be - yond the
F7 Cm7 F7 B♭ Gm
night. He still finds the time to hear a
bend. He can touch a tree and turn the
Cm7 F7 Cm7
child's first prayer, Saint or sin - ner
leaves to gold, He knows ev - 'ry

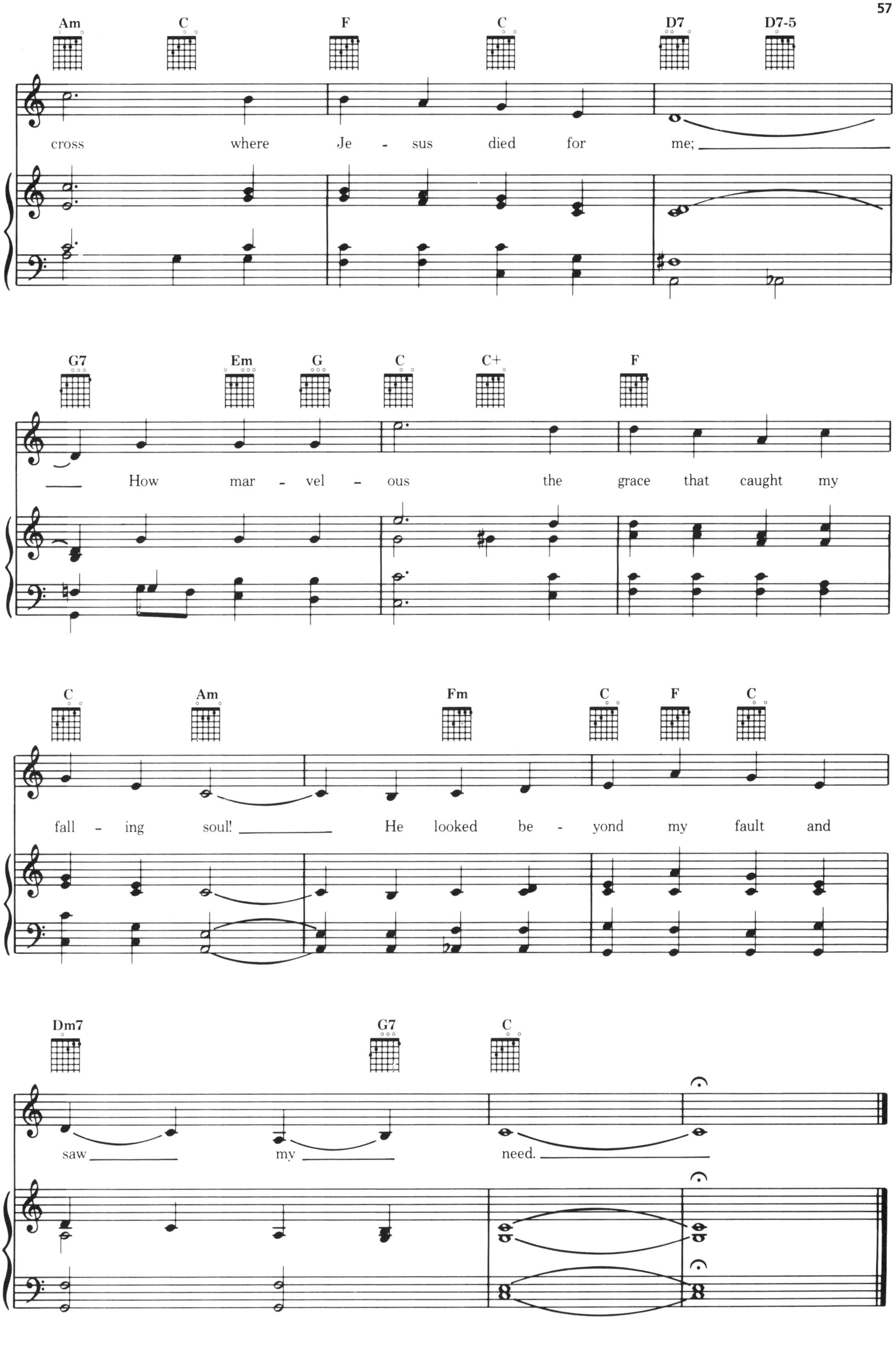
Am C F C D7 D7-5
cross where Je - sus died for me;
G7 Em G C C+ F
How mar - vel - ous the grace that caught my
C Am Fm C F C
fall - ing soul! He looked be - yond my fault and
Dm7 G7 C
saw my need.

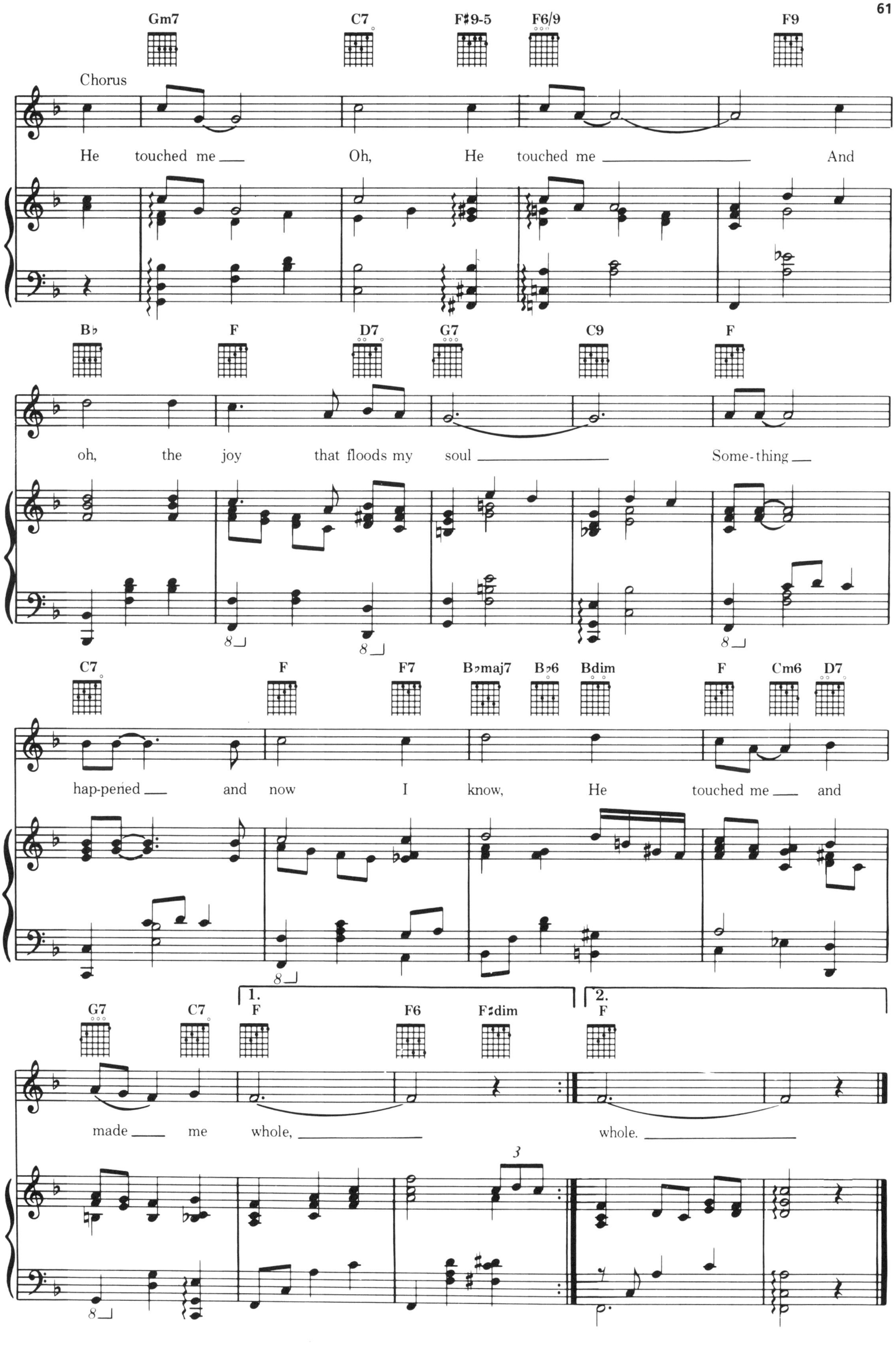
Chorus
Gm7 C7 F♯9-5 F6/9 F9
He touched me Oh, He touched me And
B♭ F D7 G7 C9 F
oh, the joy that floods my soul Some-thing
C7 F F7 B♭maj7 B♭6 Bdim F Cm6 D7
hap-pened and now I know, He touched me and
G7 C7 1. F F6 F♯dim 2. F
made me whole, whole.

HE'S GOT THE WHOLE WORLD IN HIS HANDS

Traditional Spiritual

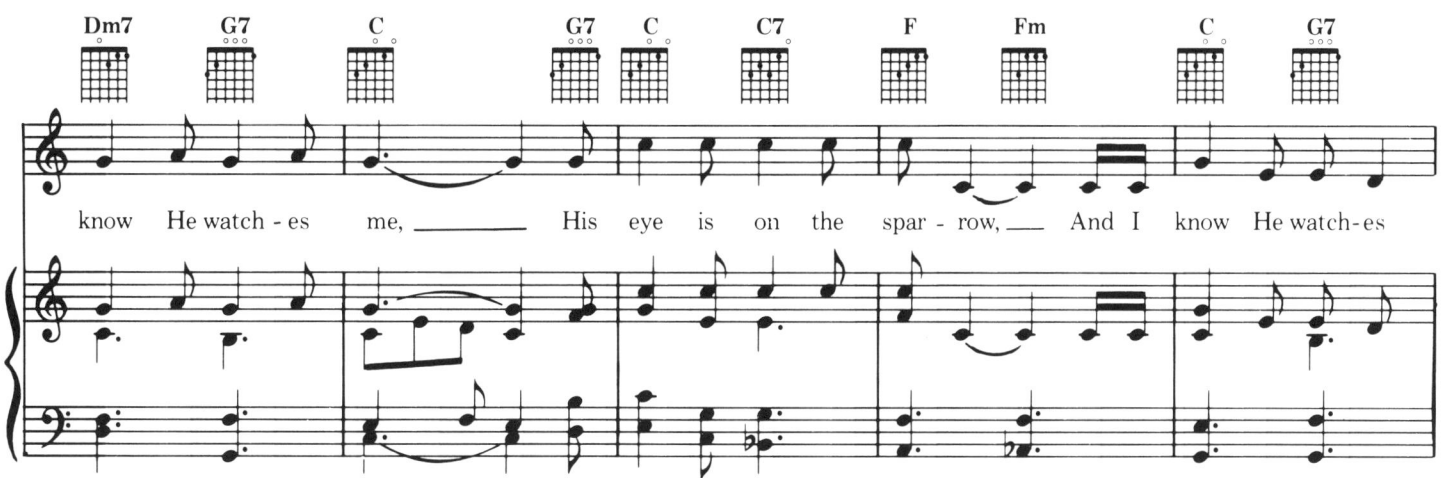

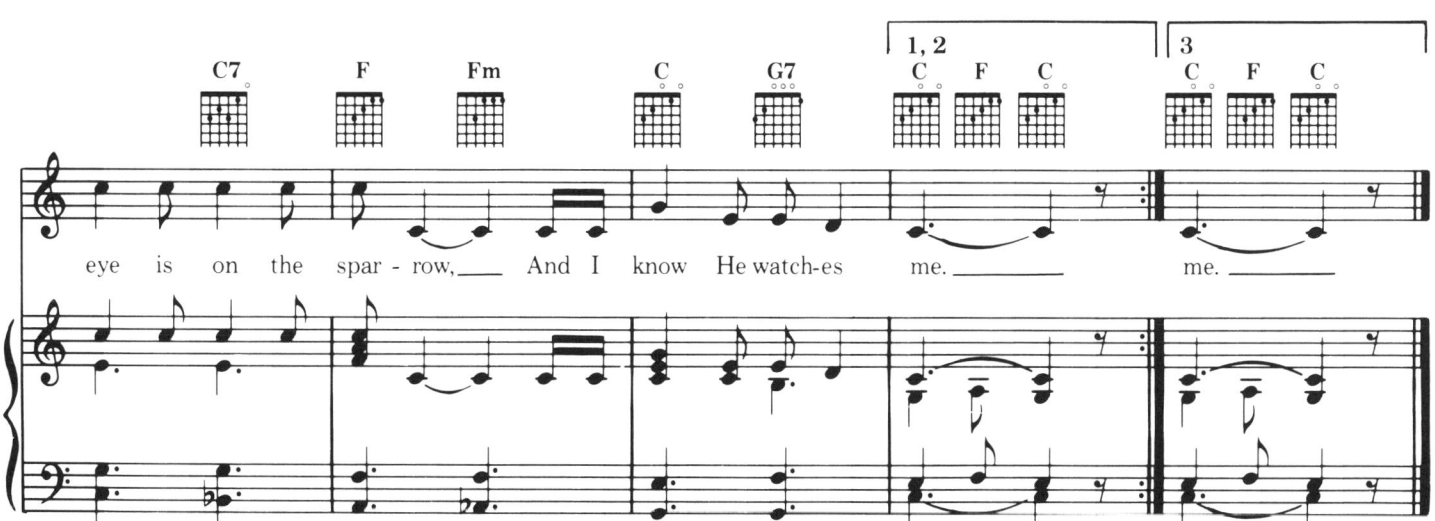

3. Whenever I am tempted,
   Whenever clouds arise.
   When song gives place to sighing,
   When hope within me dies.
   I draw the closer to Him,
   From care He sets me free:

HOLY SPIRIT, THOU ART WELCOME

By DOTTIE RAMBO
and DAVID HUNTSINGER

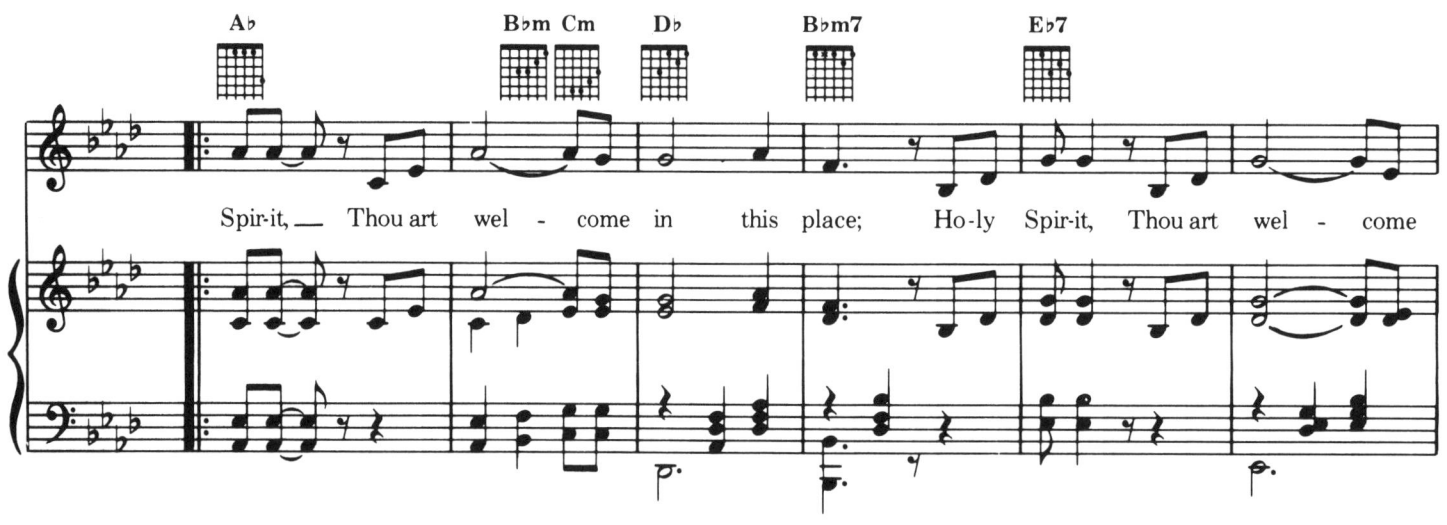
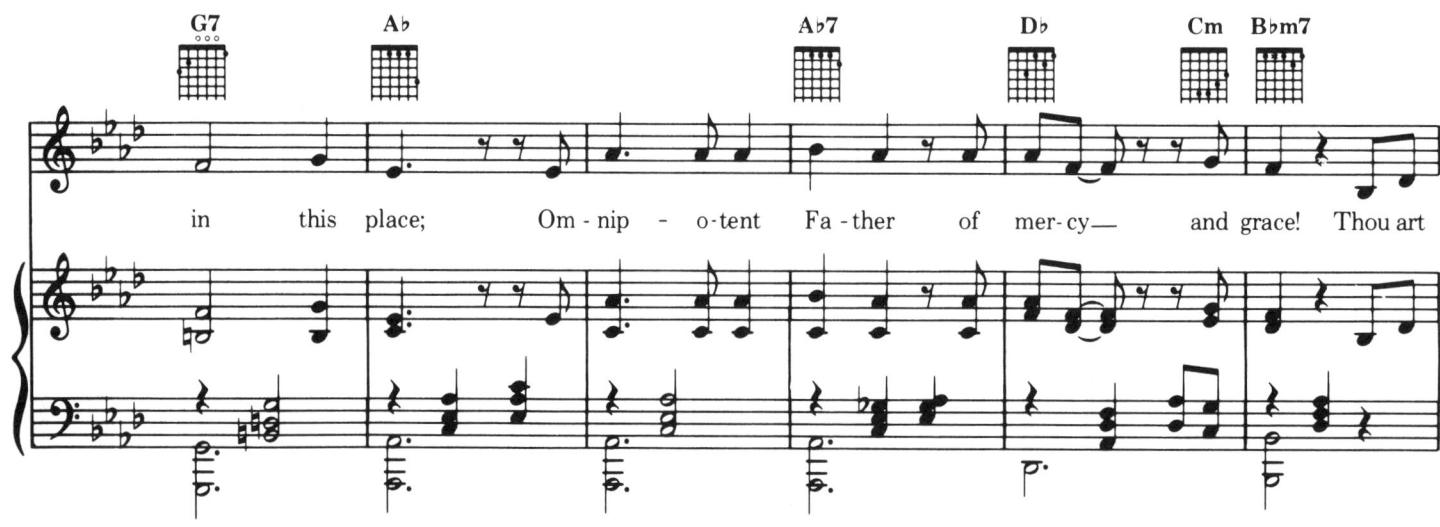

© 1977 John T. Benson Publishing Co. (ASCAP) and Bridge Building Music, Inc. (BMI) (both admin. by Brentwood-Benson Music Publishing, Inc.)
All Rights Reserved   Used by Permission

HOW GREAT THOU ART

Words and Music by
STUART K. HINE

© Copyright 1953 (Renewed 1981) by MANNA MUSIC, INC., 35255 Brooten Road, Pacific City, OR 97135
All Rights Reserved   Used by Permission

3. And when I think that God, His Son not sparing,
   Sent Him to die, I scarce can take it in;
   That on the cross, my burden gladly bearing,
   He bled and died to take away my sin;

4. When Christ shall come with shout of acclamation
   And take me home, what joy shall fill my heart!
   Then I shall bow in humble adoration
   And there proclaim, my God, How great Thou art!

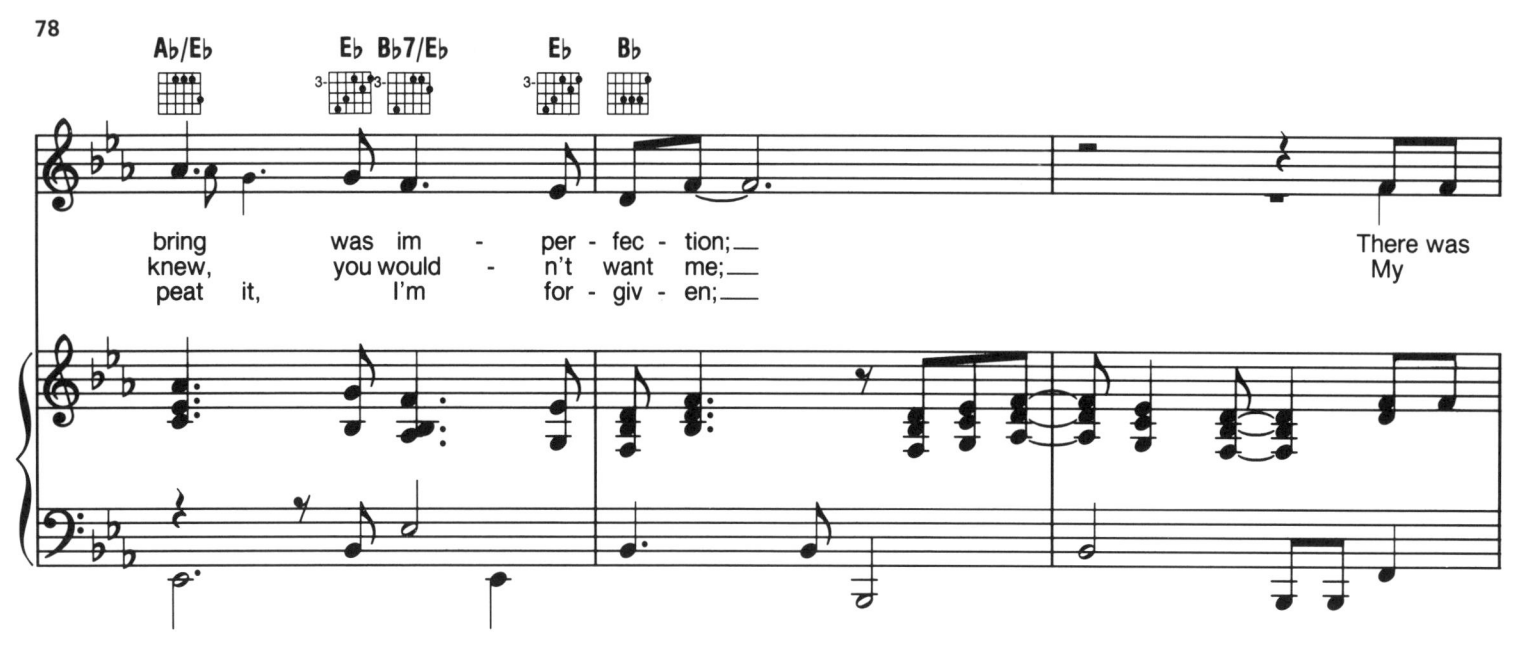

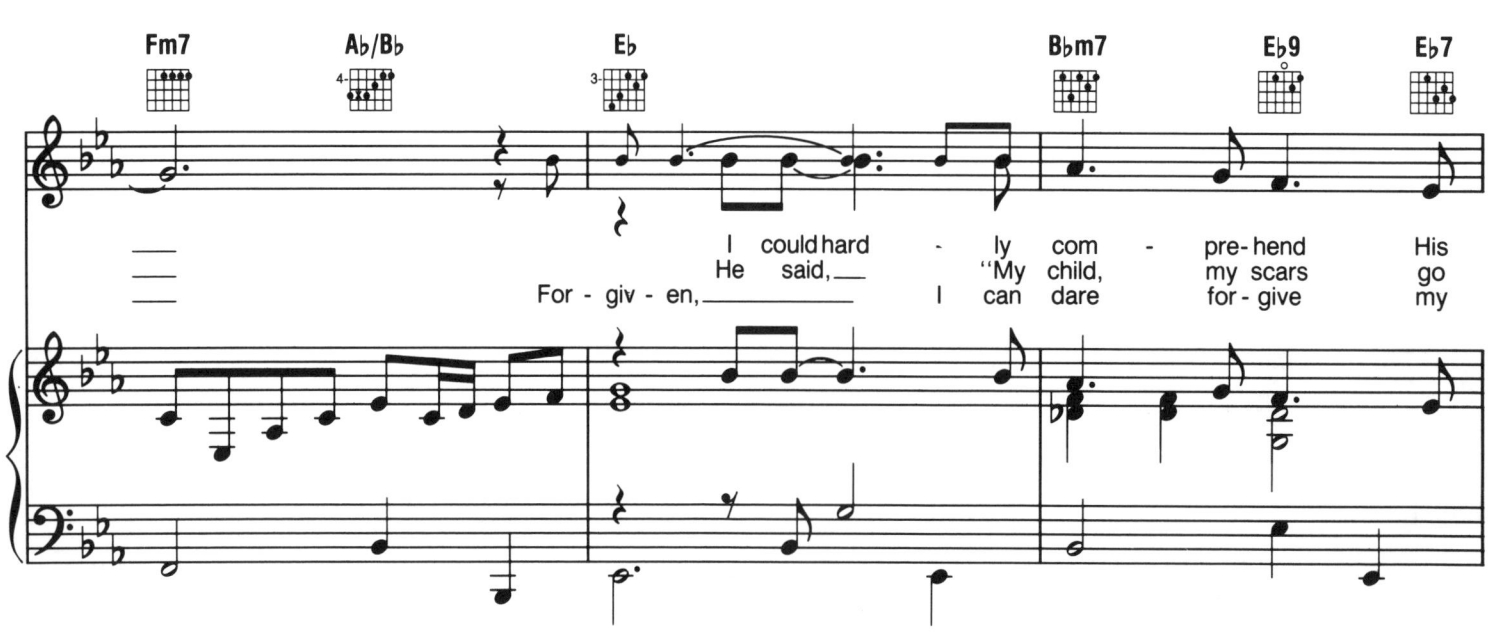

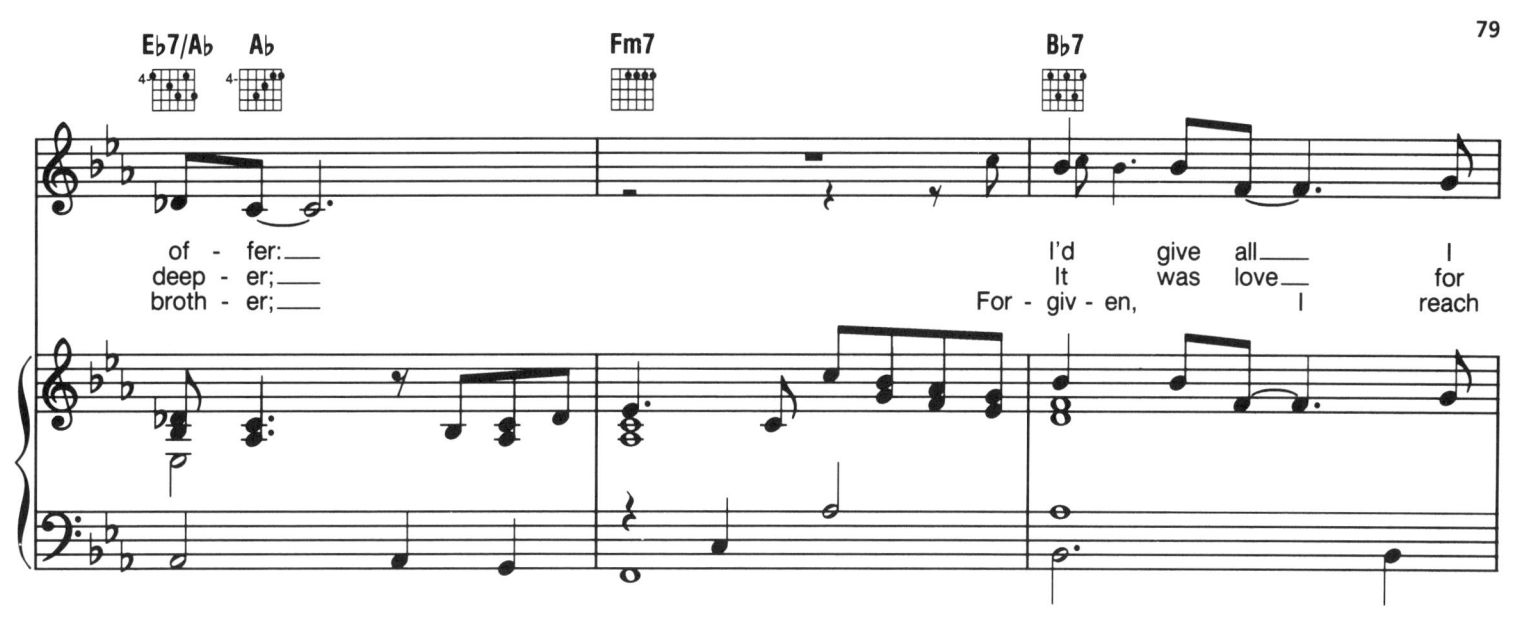
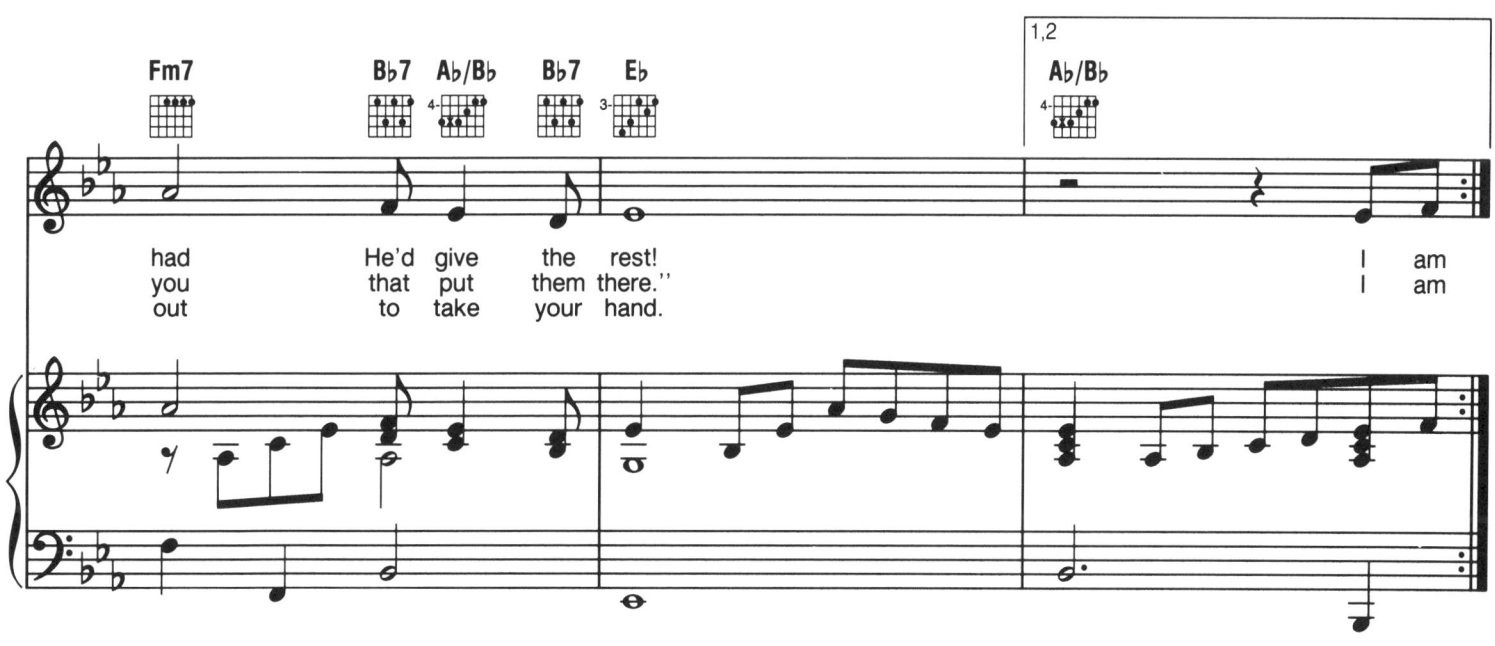
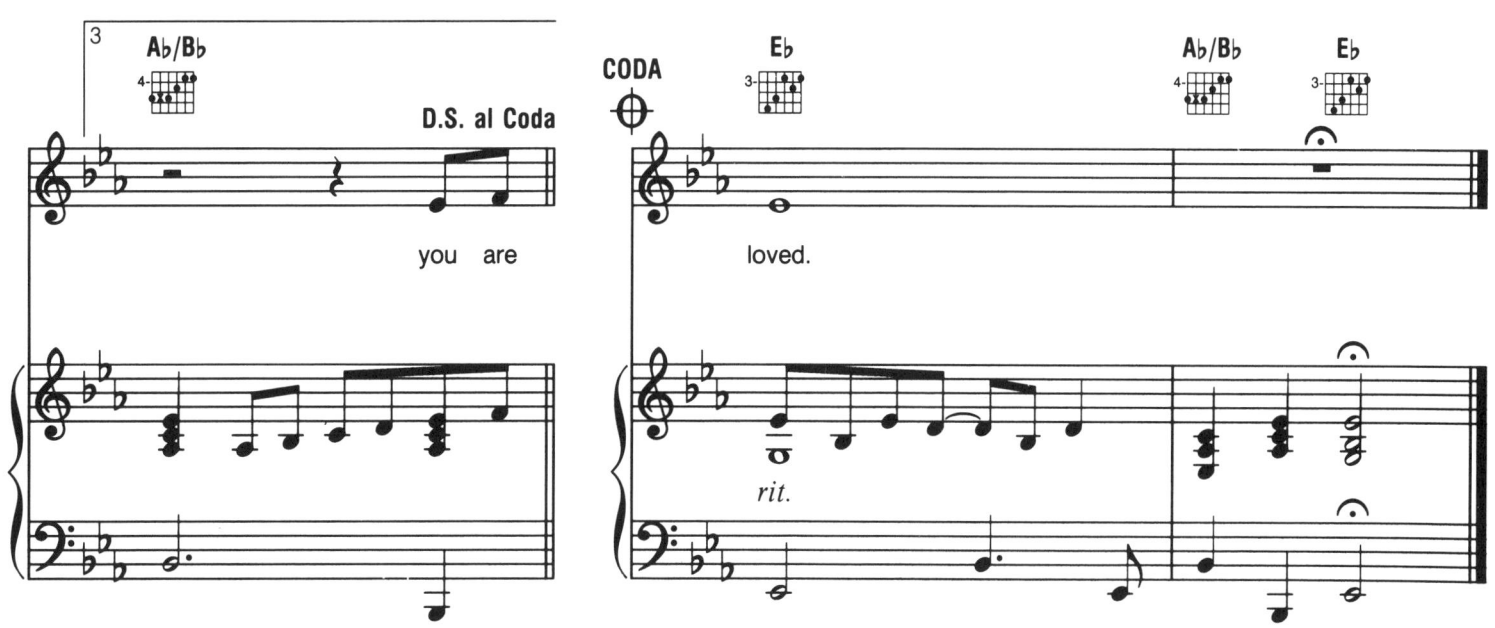

I AM NOT ASHAMED

Words and Music by
CONSTANT CHANGE

* Melody is written one octave higher than sung.

Copyright © 1990 Lehsem Music, LLC
Administered by Music & Media International, Inc.
International Copyright Secured All Rights Reserved

84

I SAW THE LIGHT

Words and Music by
HANK WILLIAMS

I WILL SERVE THEE

Words by WILLIAM J. and GLORIA GAITHER
Music by WILLIAM J. GAITHER

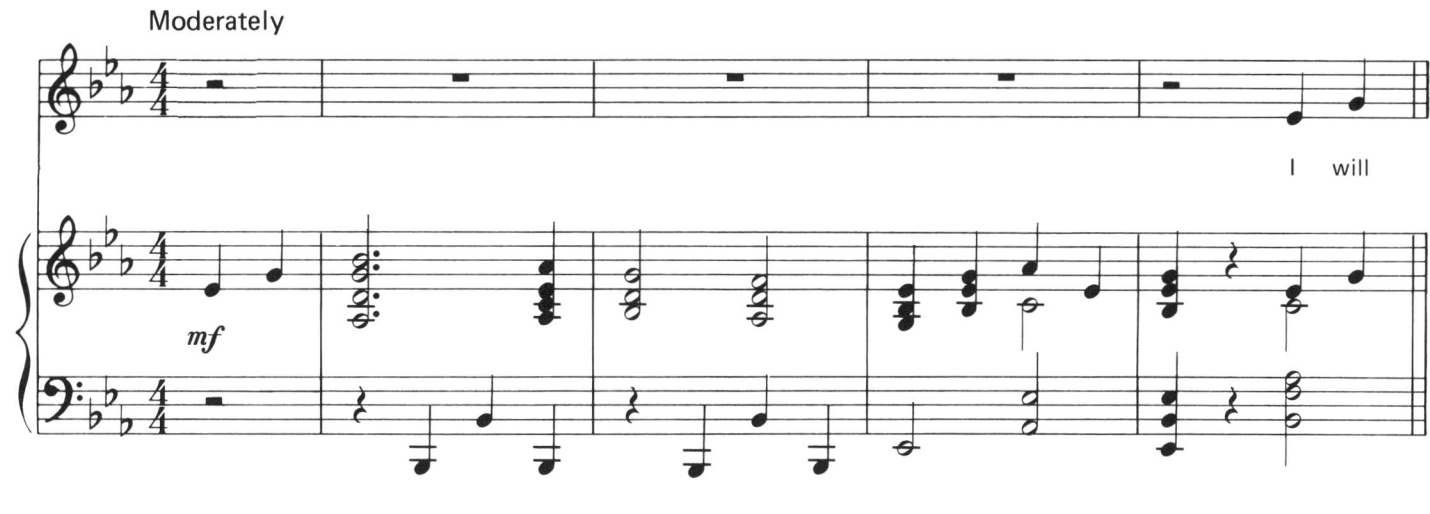

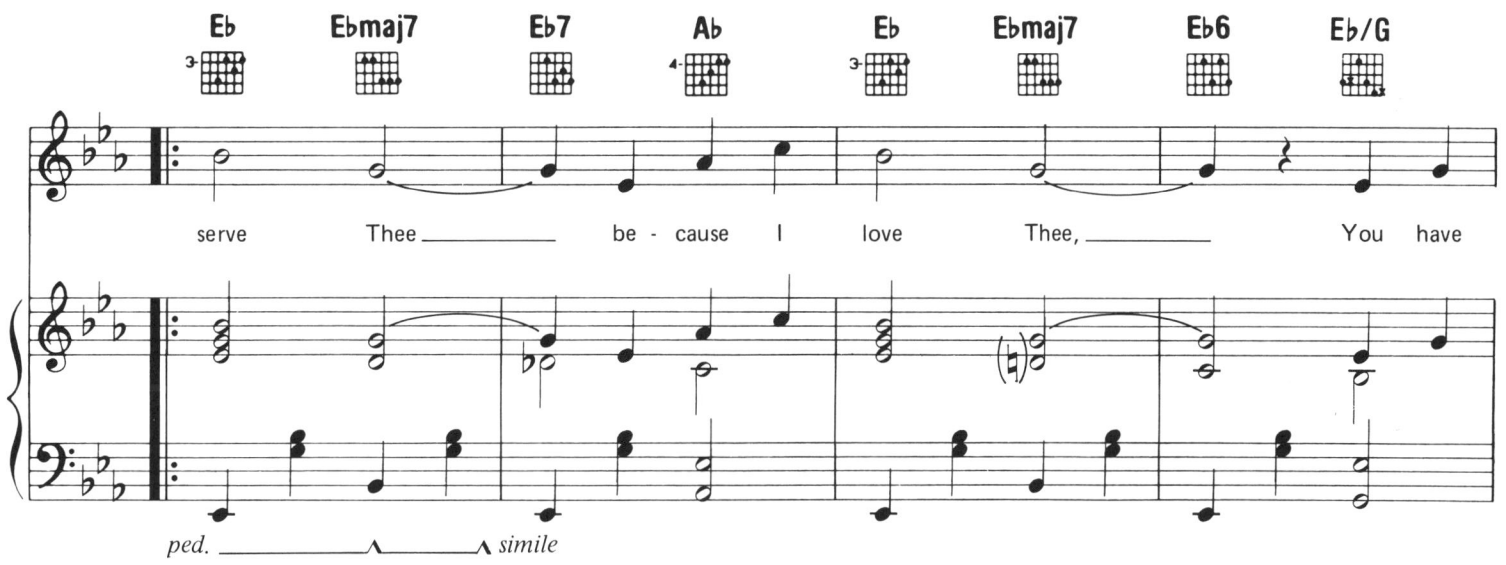

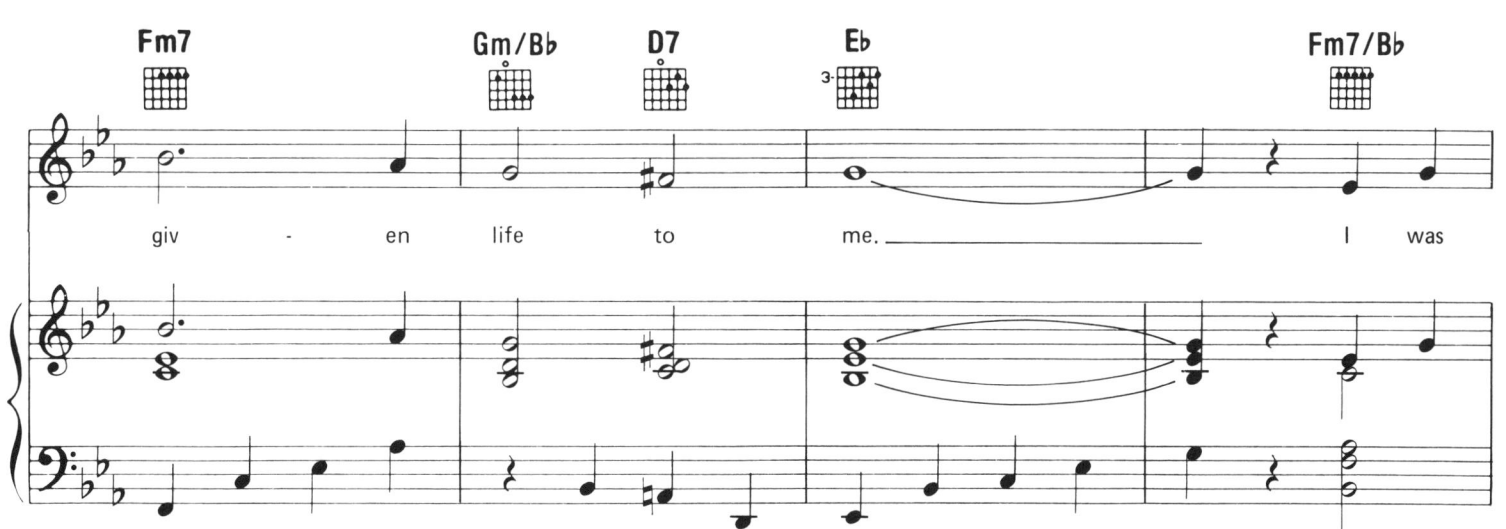

Copyright © 1969 (Renewed) William J. Gaither, Inc. (ASCAP)
All Rights Controlled by Gaither Copyright Management
All Rights Reserved   Used by Permission

I'D RATHER HAVE JESUS

Words by RHEA F. MILLER
Music by GEORGE BEVERLY SHEA

© 1922 (Renewed 1950); Music © 1939 (Renewed 1966) Word Music, Inc.
All Rights Reserved   Used by Permission

I'LL FLY AWAY

Words and Music by
ALBERT E. BRUMLEY

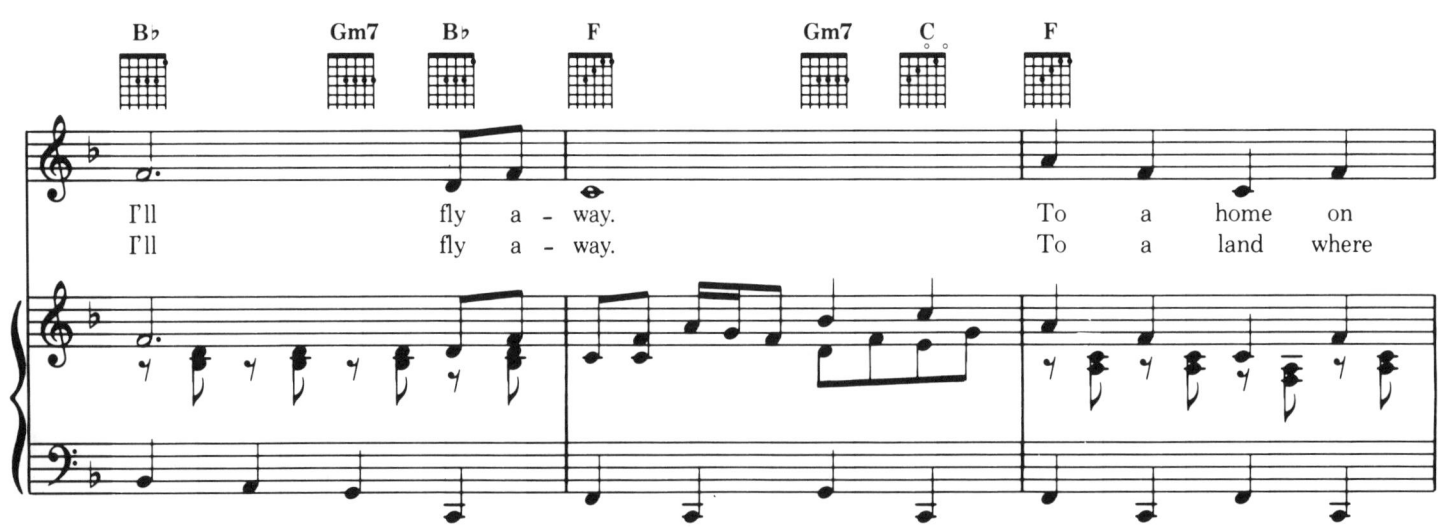

© Copyright 1932 in "Wonderful Message" by Hartford Music Company
Renewed 1960 Albert E. Brumley & Sons (SESAC)/admin. by ICG
All Rights Reserved   Used by Permission

3. Now I'm pressing onward,,
   Each step leads me homeward,
   I'm trusting in my Savior day by day;
   And close is our relation,
   Firm is it's foundation,
   So on this Solid Rock I'll stay.

IN THE GARDEN

Words and Music by
C. AUSTIN MILES

JESUS PAID IT ALL

Words by ELVINA M. HALL
Music by JOHN T. GRAPE

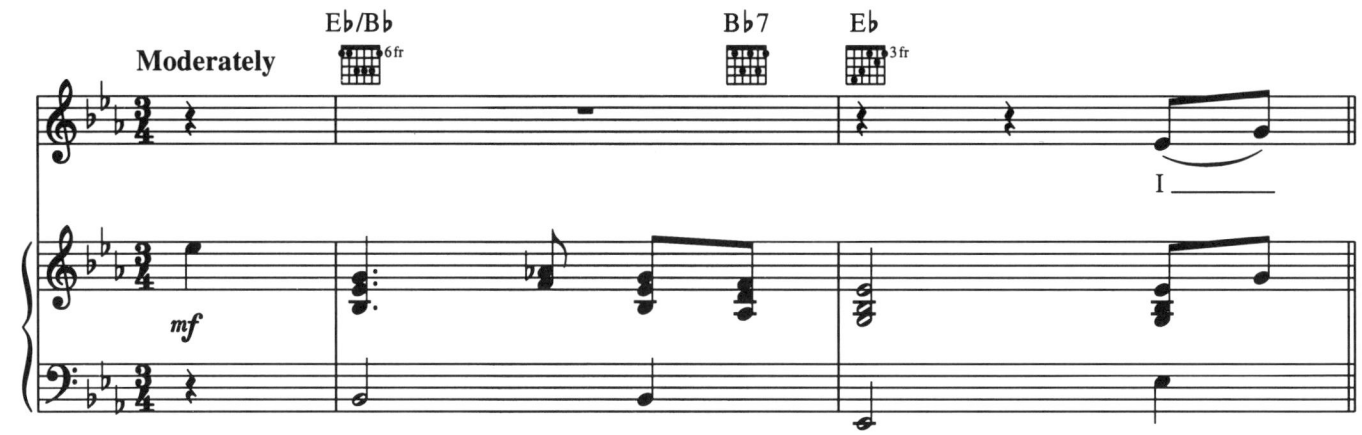

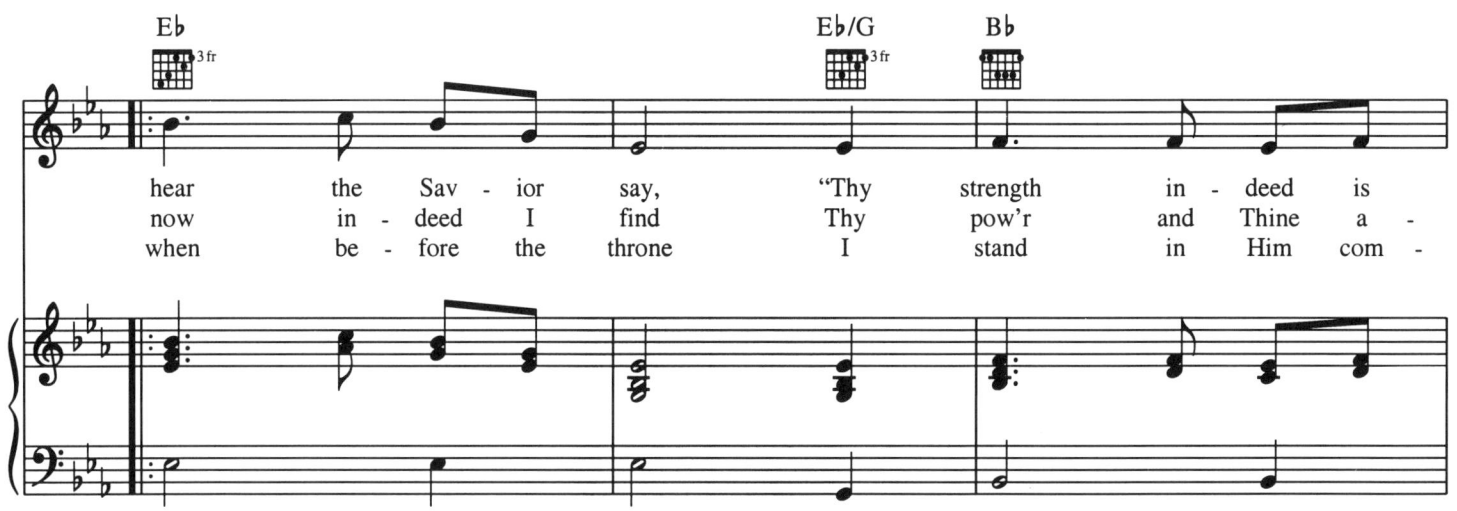

hear the Sav - ior say, "Thy strength in - deed is
now in - deed I find Thy pow'r and Thine a -
when be - fore the throne I stand in Him com -

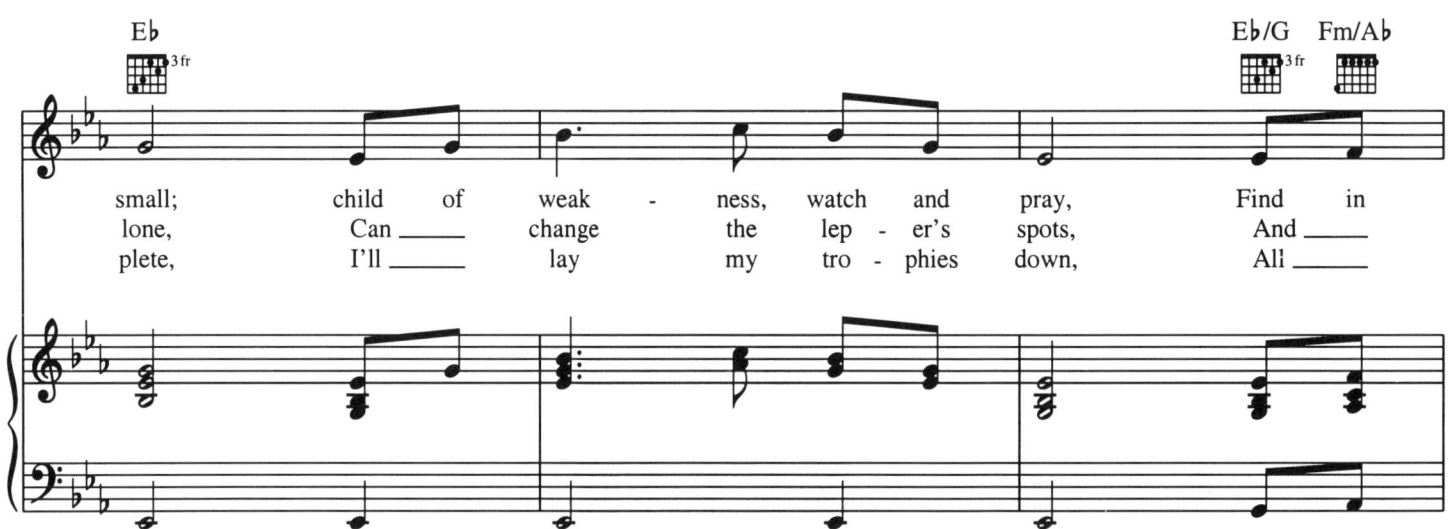

small; child of weak - ness, watch and pray, Find in
lone, Can change the lep - er's spots, And
plete, I'll lay my tro - phies down, All

Copyright © 1997 by HAL LEONARD CORPORATION
International Copyright Secured   All Rights Reserved

JUST A LITTLE TALK WITH JESUS

Words and Music by
CLEAVANT DERRICKS

© 1937 Stamps-Baxter Music (BMI) (admin. by Brentwood-Benson Music Publishing, Inc.)
Copyright Renewed
All Rights Reserved   Used by Permission

LAMB OF GLORY

Words and Music by GREG NELSON
and PHILL McHUGH

Moderately flowing

Hear the sto-ry from God's word that kings and priests and pro-phets heard.

© 1982 RIVER OAKS MUSIC COMPANY and SHEPHERD'S FOLD MUSIC
Admin. by EMI CHRISTIAN MUSIC PUBLISHING
All Rights Reserved   Used by Permission

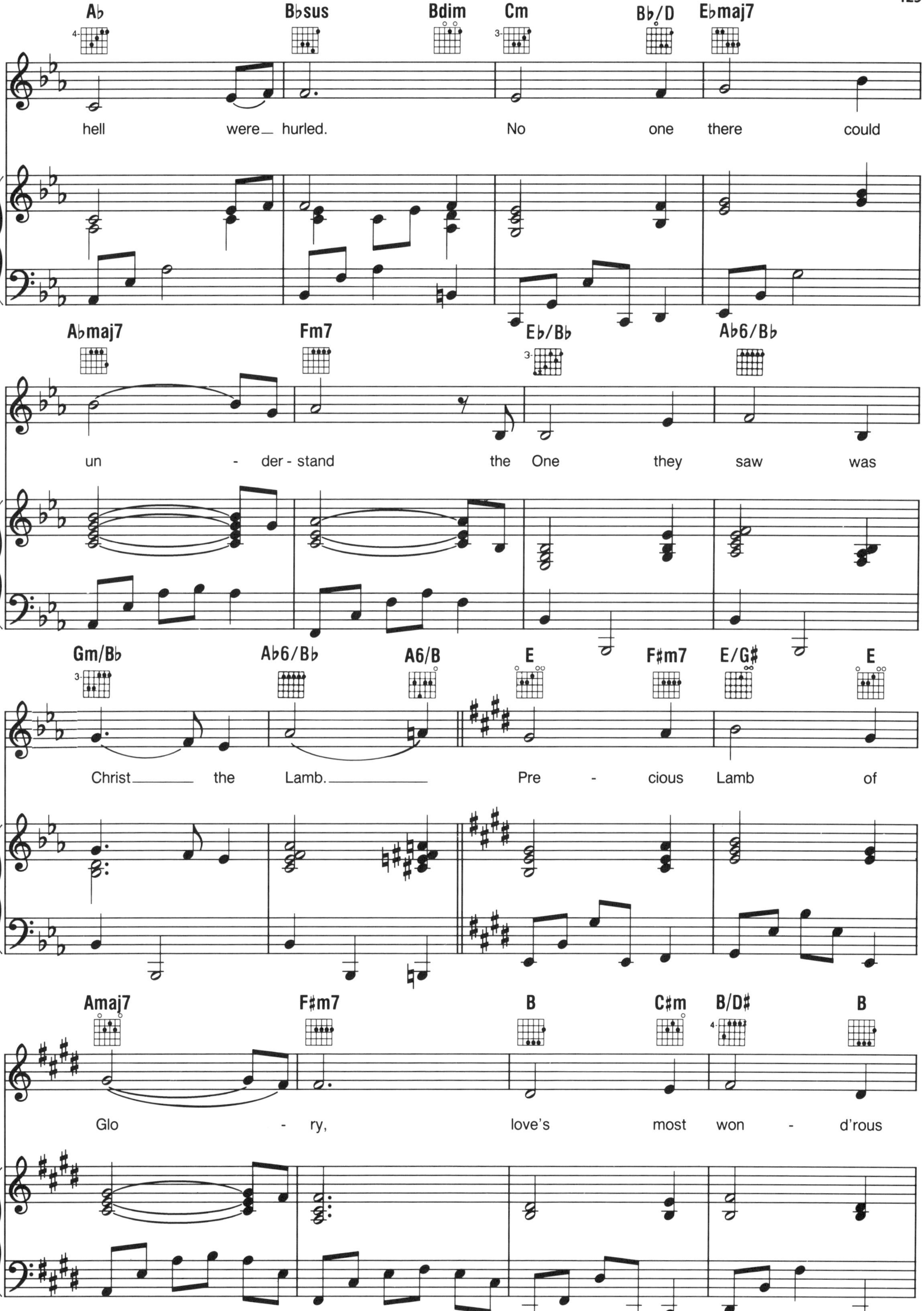

A♭ B♭sus Bdim Cm B♭/D E♭maj7
hell were hurled. No one there could
A♭maj7 Fm7 E♭/B♭ A♭6/B♭
un - der- stand the One they saw was
Gm/B♭ A♭6/B♭ A6/B E F♯m7 E/G♯ E
Christ the Lamb. Pre - cious Lamb of
Amaj7 F♯m7 B C♯m B/D♯ B
Glo - ry, love's most won - d'rous

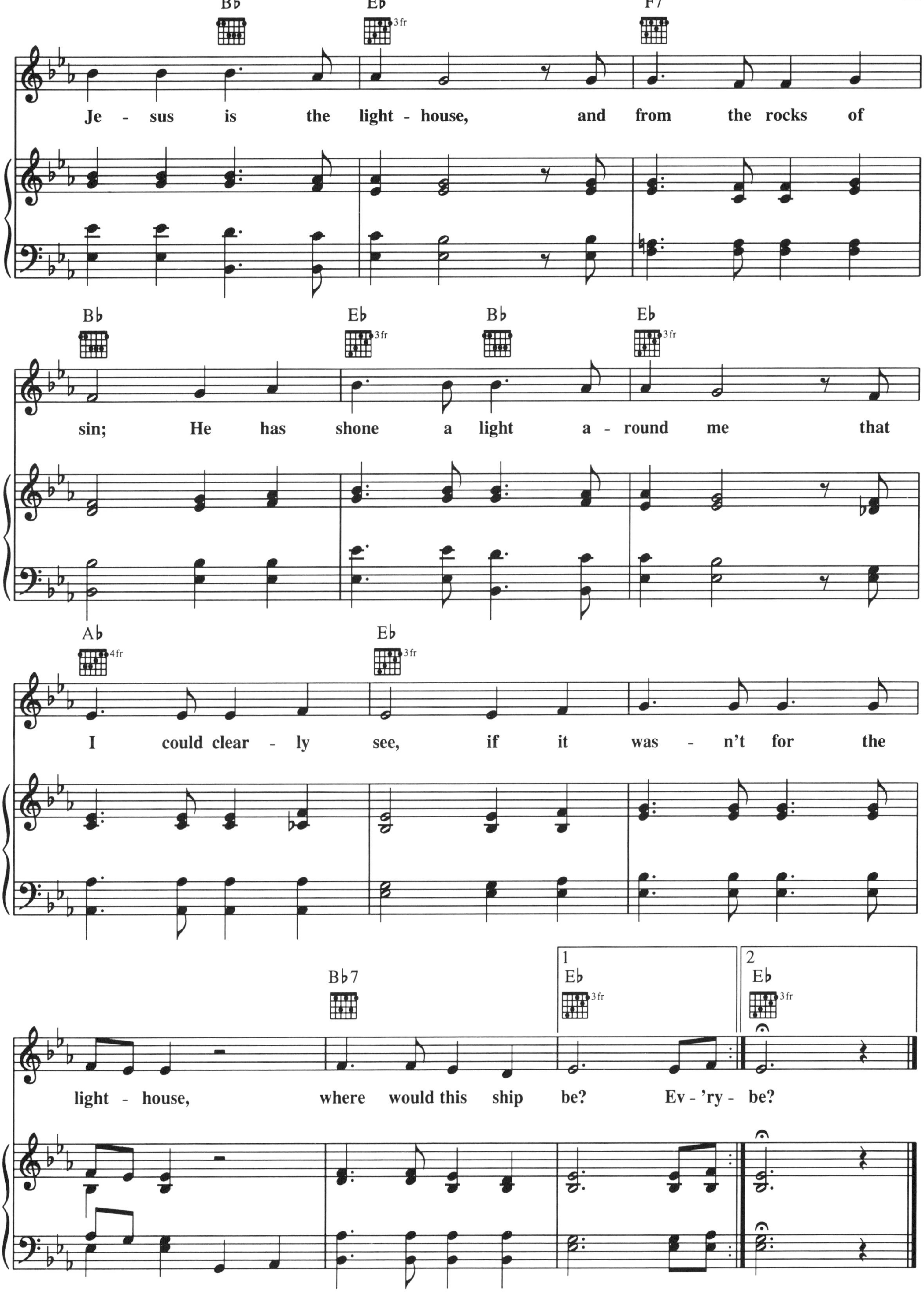
B♭ E♭ F7
Je - sus is the light - house, and from the rocks of
B♭ E♭ B♭ E♭
sin; He has shone a light a - round me that
A♭ E♭
I could clear - ly see, if it was - n't for the
B♭7 1 E♭ 2 E♭
light - house, where would this ship be? Ev - 'ry - be?

LIFE'S RAILWAY TO HEAVEN

Words by M.E. ABBEY
Music by CHARLES D. TILLMAN

Copyright © 1999 by HAL LEONARD CORPORATION
International Copyright Secured   All Rights Reserved

THE LILY OF THE VALLEY

Words by CHARLES W. FRY
Music by WILLIAM S. HAYS

Moderately

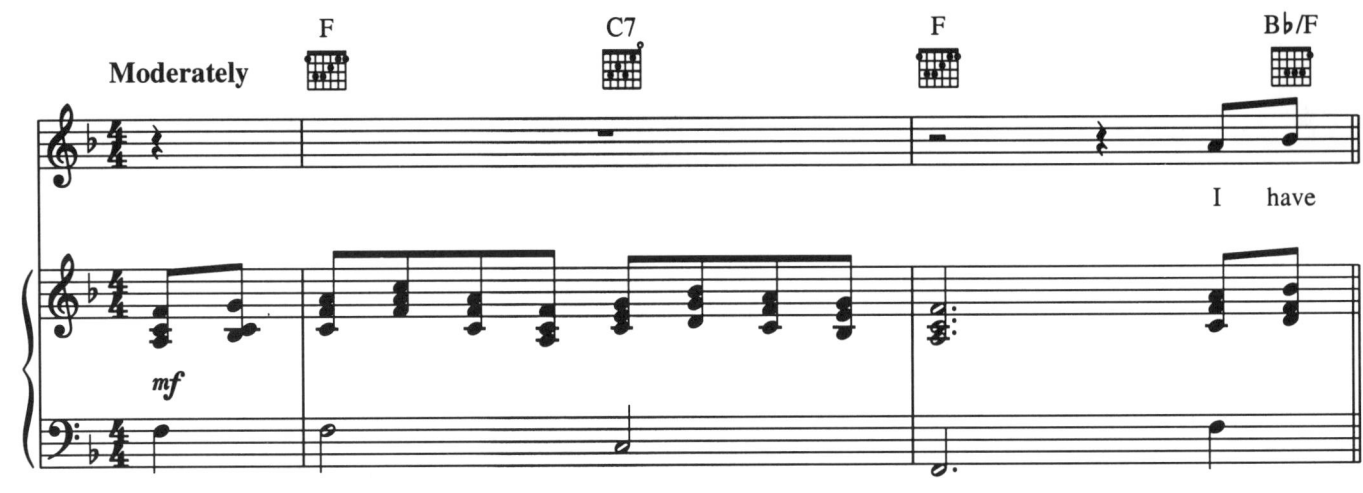

I have
found a friend in Jesus, He's ev-'ry-thing to me, He's the
all my grief has tak-en, and all my sor-rows borne; In temp-
nev-er, nev-er leave me, nor yet for-sake me here, While I

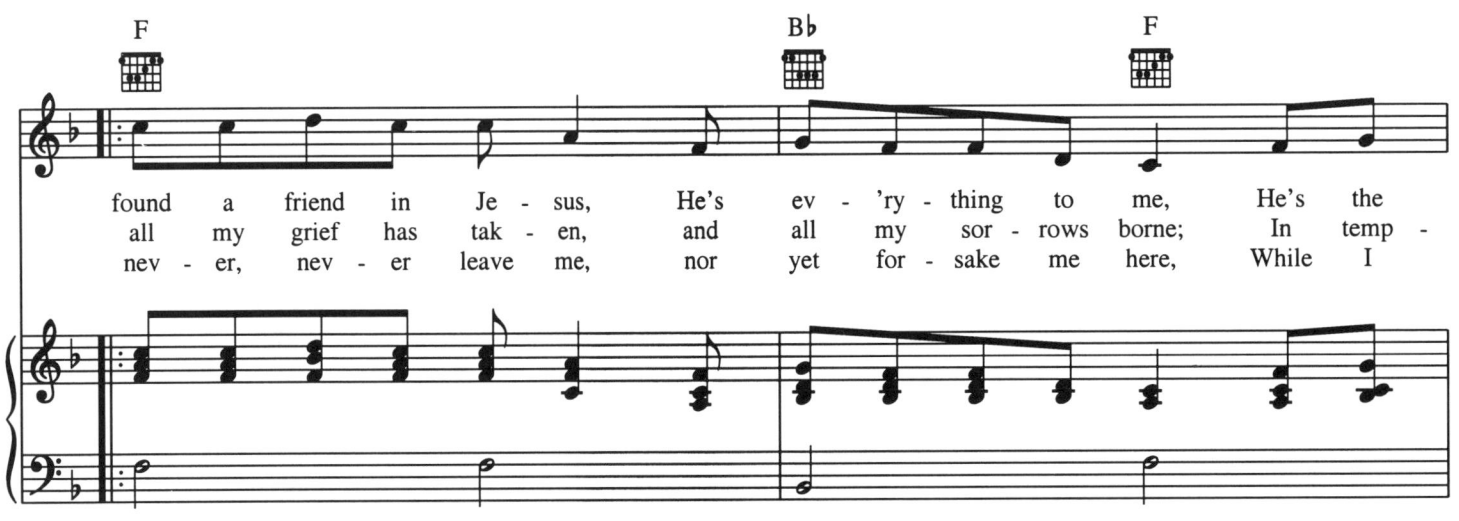

fair-est of ten-thou-sand to my soul; The Lil-y of the Val-ley, in
ta-tion He's my strong and might-y tower; I have all for Him for-sak-en, and
live by faith and do His bless-ed will; A wall of fire a-bout me, I've

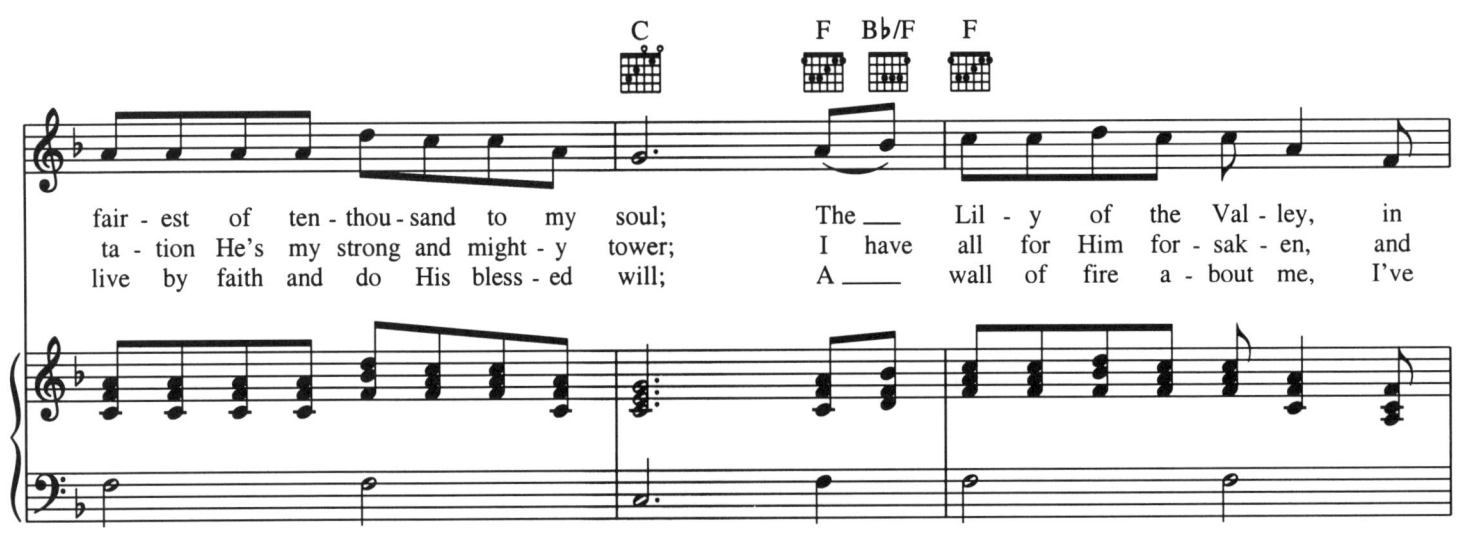

Copyright © 1997 by HAL LEONARD CORPORATION
International Copyright Secured   All Rights Reserved

LITTLE IS MUCH WHEN GOD IS IN IT

Words by MRS. F.W. SUFFIELD and DWIGHT BROCK
Music by MRS. F.W. SUFFIELD

THE LONGER I SERVE HIM

Words and Music by
WILLIAM J. GAITHER

Copyright © 1965 (Renewed) William J. Gaither, Inc. (ASCAP)
All Rights Controlled by Gaither Copyright Management
All Rights Reserved   Used by Permission

LOVE LIFTED ME

Words by JAMES ROWE
Music by HOWARD E. SMITH

THE LOVE OF GOD

Words and Music by
FREDERICK M. LEHMAN

MANSION OVER THE HILLTOP

Words and Music by
IRA F. STANPHILL

© 1949 Singspiration Music (ASCAP) (admin. by Brentwood-Benson Music Publishing, Inc.)
Copyright Renewed
All Rights Reserved   Used by Permission

MORE THAN WONDERFUL

Words and Music by
LANNY WOLFE

real for I can feel Him deep with-in.
real and I can feel Him in my heart.
real for I can feel His ho-ly power.
Yes, God is real, real in my soul. Yes, God is real for He has washed and made me whole. His love for me is like pure gold. Yes, God is real for I can feel Him in my soul.

Some folk may
I can-not soul.

MY TRIBUTE

Words and Music by
ANDRAÉ CROUCH

© 1971 (Renewed) BUD JOHN SONGS, INC.
Admin. by EMI CHRISTIAN MUSIC PUBLISHING
All Rights Reserved   Used by Permission

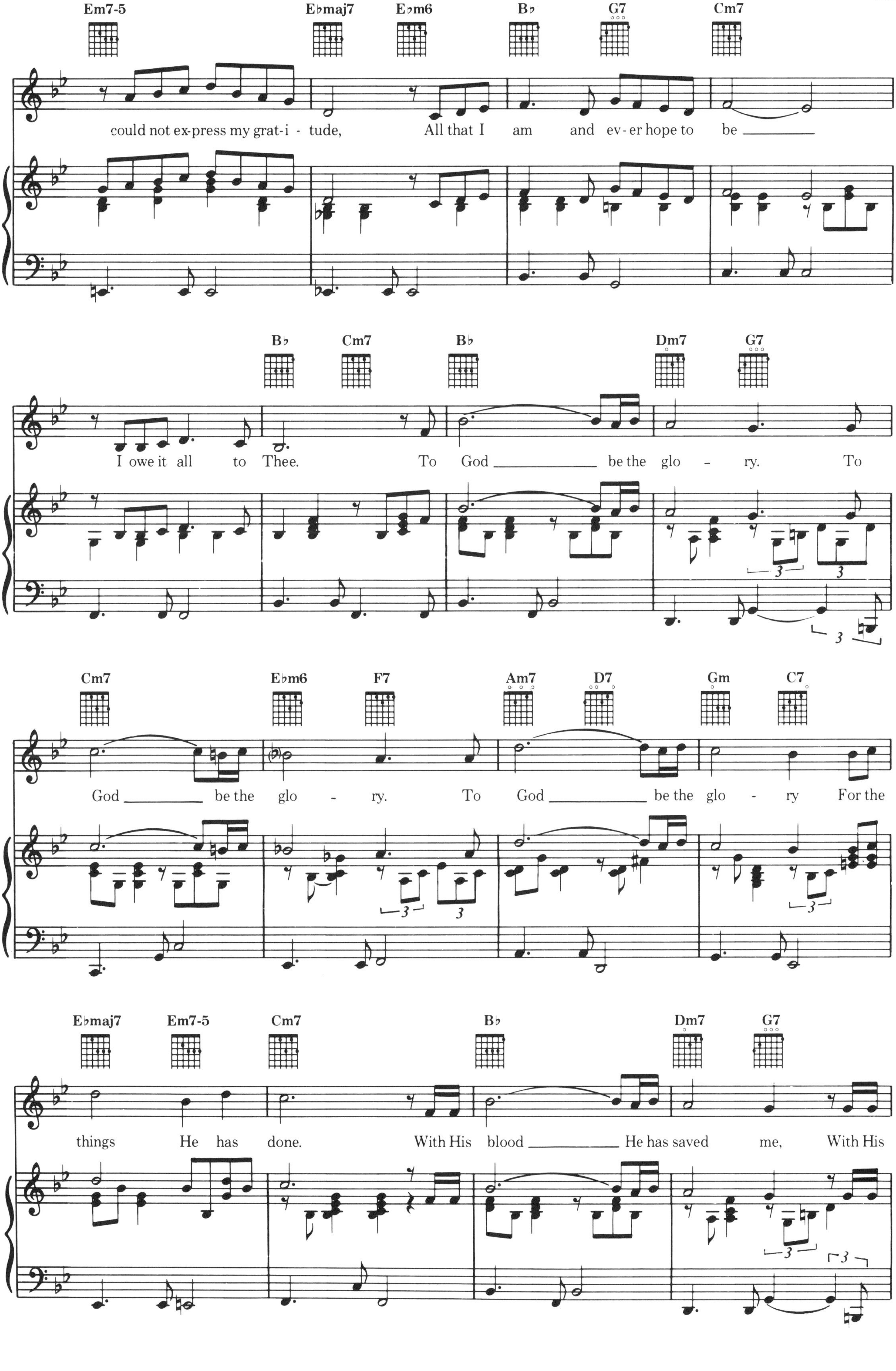
Em7-5 E♭maj7 E♭m6 B♭ G7 Cm7
could not ex-press my grat-i - tude, All that I am and ev-er hope to be
B♭ Cm7 B♭ Dm7 G7
I owe it all to Thee. To God be the glo - ry. To
Cm7 E♭m6 F7 Am7 D7 Gm C7
God be the glo - ry. To God be the glo - ry For the
E♭maj7 Em7-5 Cm7 B♭ Dm7 G7
things He has done. With His blood He has saved me, With His

A New Name In Glory

Words and Music by
C. AUSTIN MILES

OH, HOW I LOVE JESUS

Words by FREDERICK WHITFIELD
Traditional American Melody

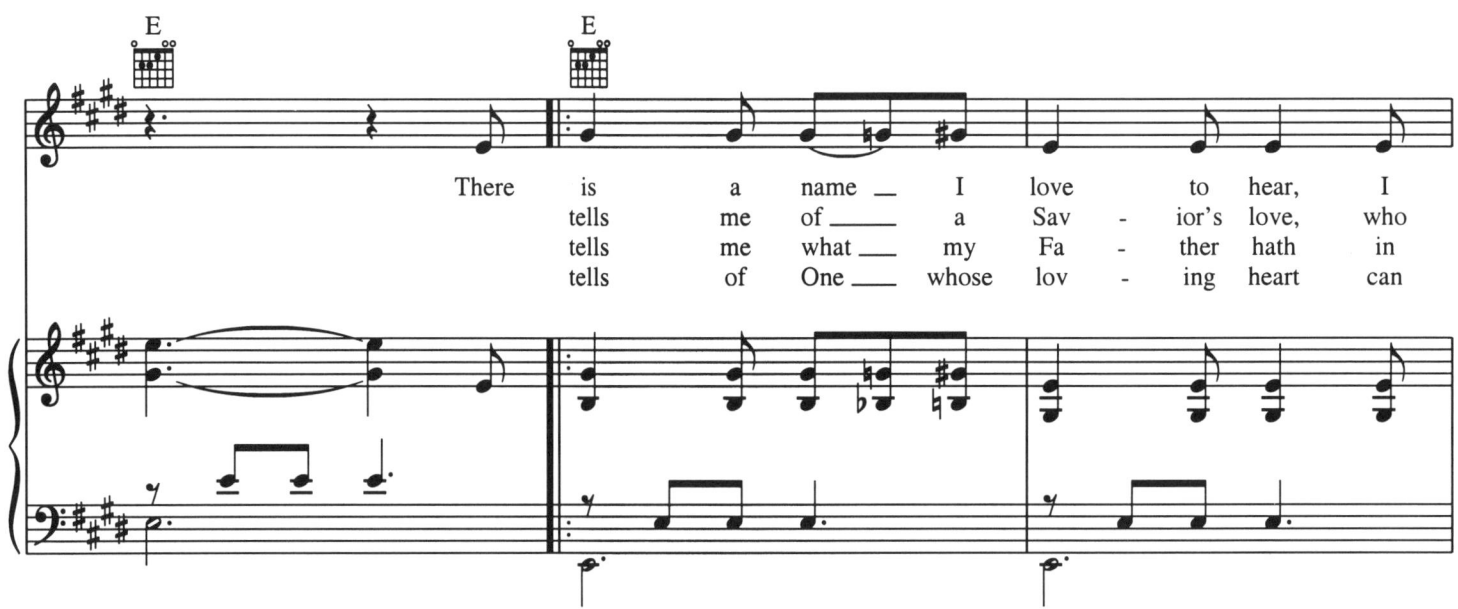

THE OLD RUGGED CROSS

Words and Music by
REV. GEORGE BENNARD

Copyright © 1983 by HAL LEONARD CORPORATION
International Copyright Secured All Rights Reserved

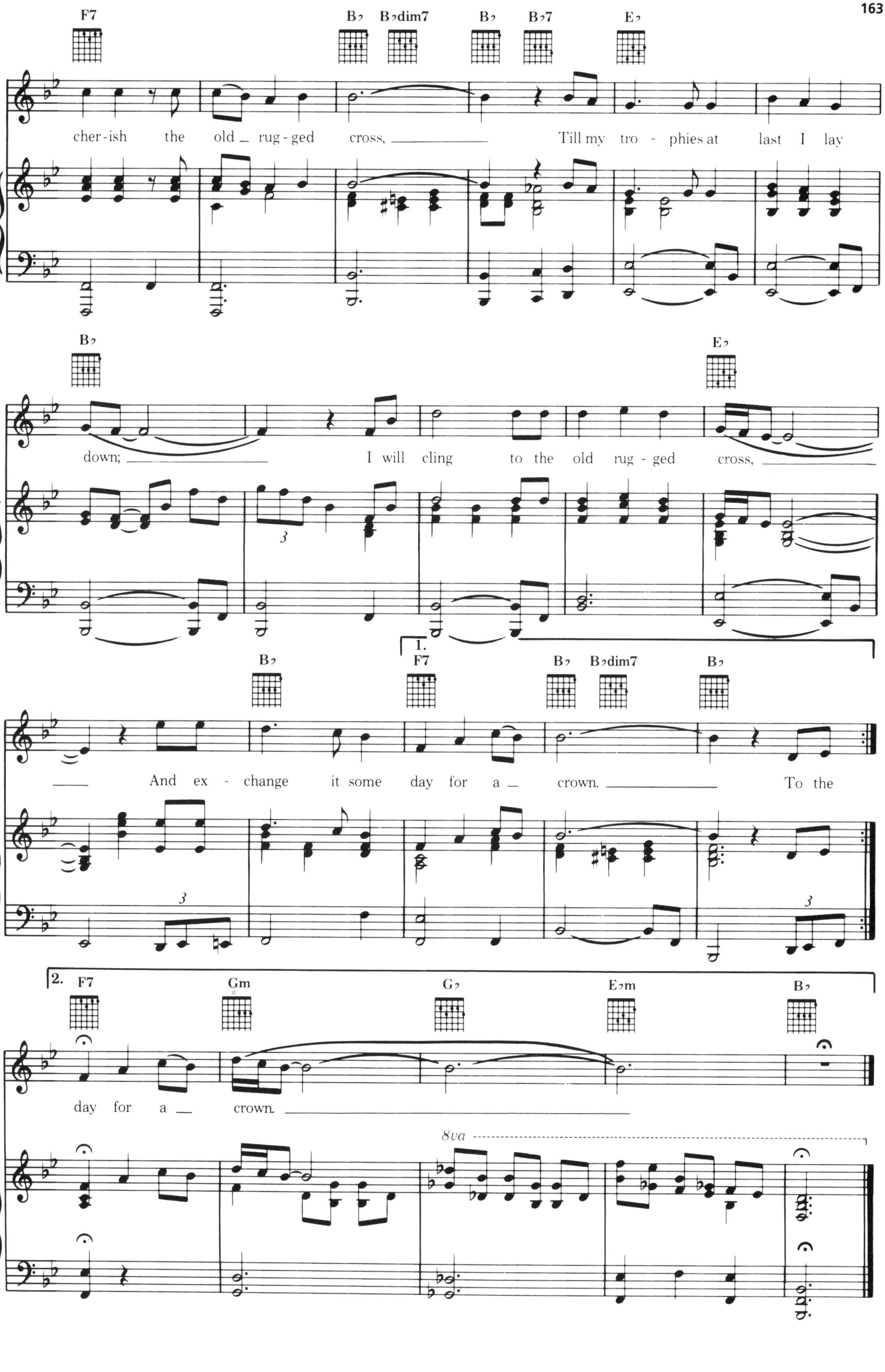
F7 B♭ B♭dim7 B♭ B♭7 E♭
cher-ish the old rug-ged cross, Till my tro - phies at last I lay
B♭ E♭
down; I will cling to the old rug - ged cross,
B♭ 1. F7 B♭ B♭dim7 B♭
And ex - change it some day for a crown. To the
2. F7 Gm G♭ E♭m B♭
day for a crown.
8va

ON JORDAN'S STORMY BANKS

Words by SAMUEL STENNETT
Traditional American Melody

3. There the bear will be gentle, the wolf will be tame,
   And the lion will lay down by the lamb,
   The host from the wild will be led by a Child,
   I'll be changed from the creature I am.

4. No headaches or heartaches or misunderstands,
   No confusion or trouble won't be,
   No frowns to defile, just a long endless smile,
   There'll be peace and contentment for me.

PRECIOUS MEMORIES

Words and Music by J.B.F. WRIGHT

3. As I travel on life's pathway, I know not what life shall hold;
As I wander hopes grow fonder, Precious mem'ries flood my soul.

PUT YOUR HAND IN THE HAND

Words and Music by
GENE MacLELLAN

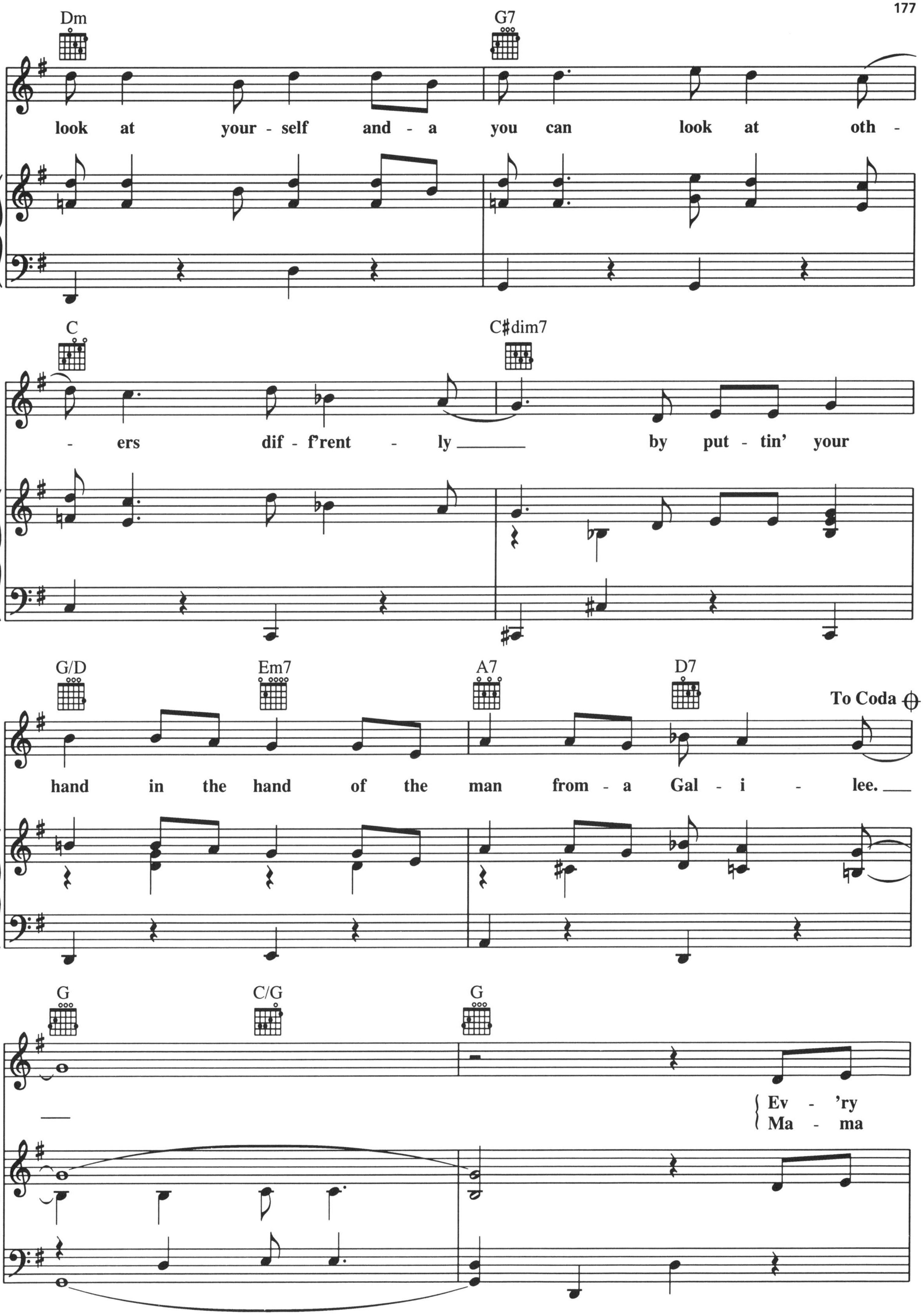
Dm
G7
look at your - self and - a you can look at oth -
C
C♯dim7
- ers dif - f'rent - ly by put - tin' your
G/D
Em7
A7
D7
To Coda
hand in the hand of the man from - a Gal - i - lee.
G
C/G
G
Ev - 'ry
Ma - ma

RISE AGAIN

Words and Music by
DALLAS HOLM

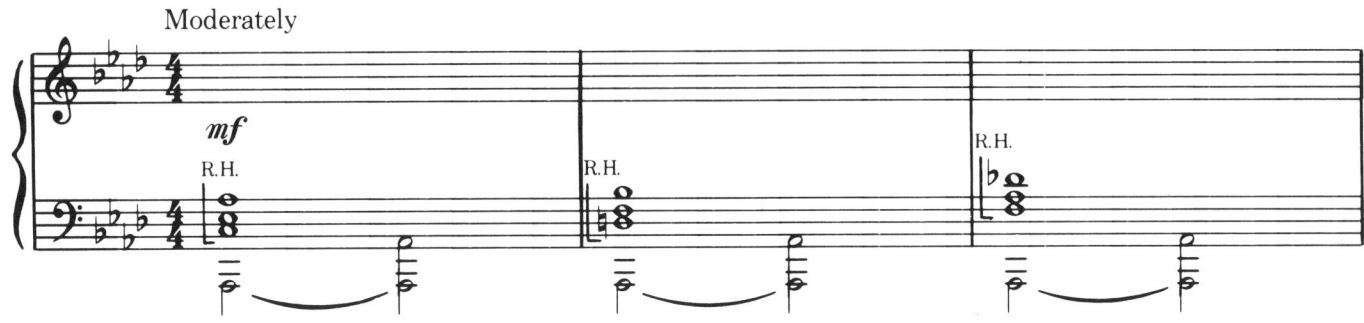
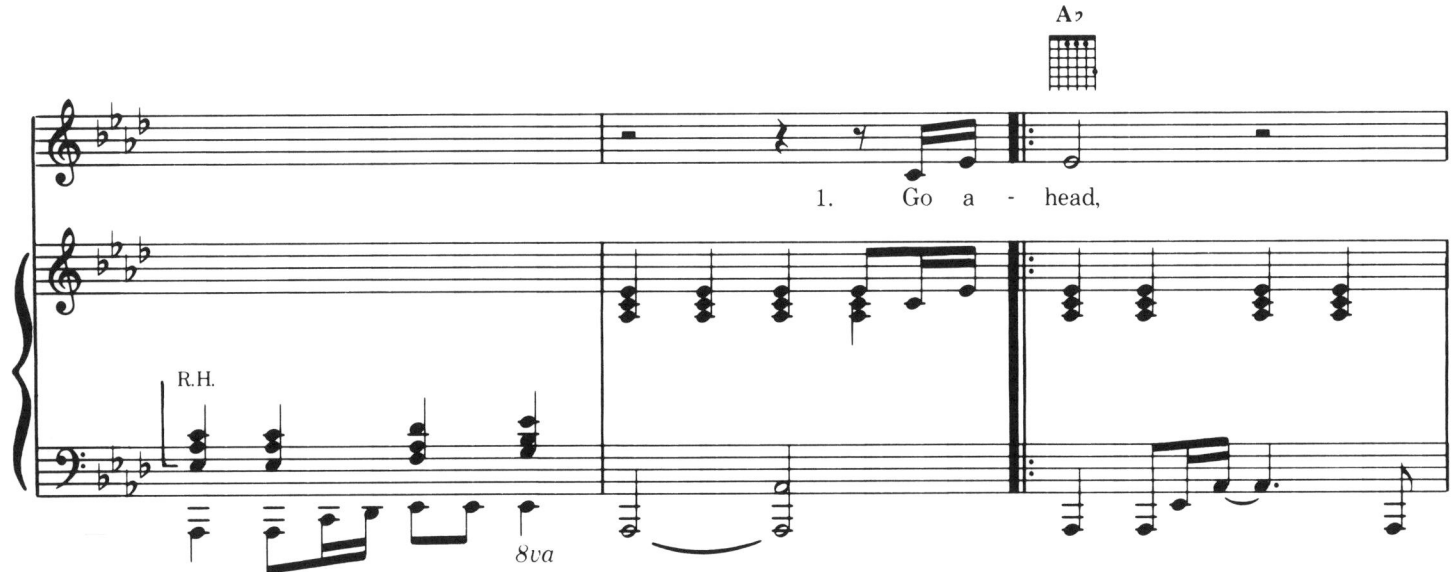

© 1977 Designer Music (SESAC) and Going Holm Music (SESAC) (both admin. by Brentwood-Benson Music Publishing, Inc.)
All Rights Reserved Used by Permission

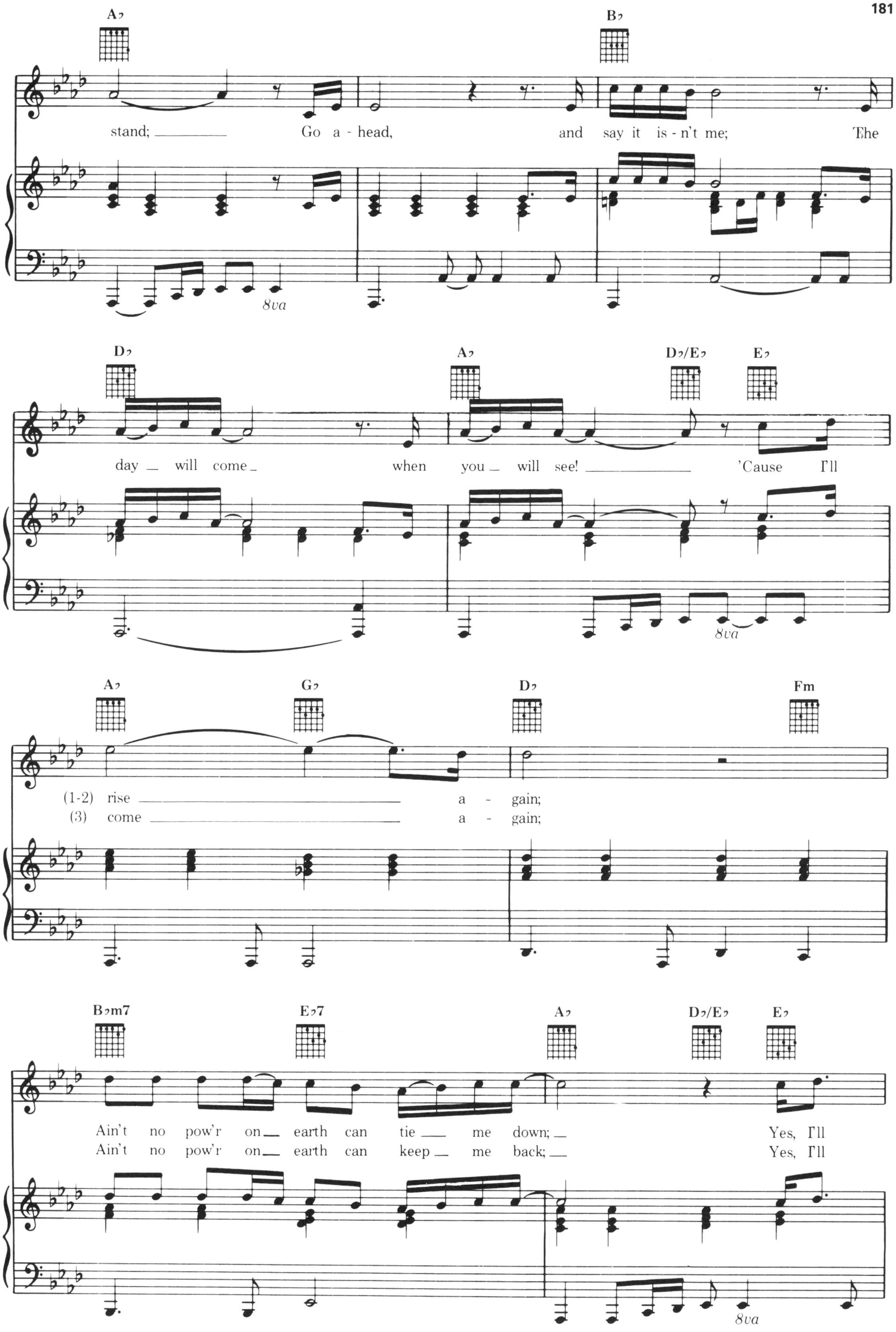
A♭
B♭
stand; Go a - head, and say it is - n't me; The
8va
D♭
A♭
D♭/E♭
E♭
day will come when you will see! 'Cause I'll
8va
A♭
G♭
D♭
Fm
(1-2) rise a - gain;
(3) come a - gain;
B♭m7
E♭7
A♭
D♭/E♭
E♭
Ain't no pow'r on earth can tie me down; Yes, I'll
Ain't no pow'r on earth can keep me back; Yes, I'll
8va

2. Go ahead, and mock my name; My love for you is still the same;
   Go ahead and bury me; But very soon I will be free!
   'Cause I'll . . . (chorus)

3. Go ahead and say I'm dead and gone, But you will see that you were wrong
   Go ahead, try to hide the Son, But all will see that I'm the One!
   'Cause I'll . . . (chorus)

SHALL WE GATHER AT THE RIVER?

Words and Music by
ROBERT LOWRY

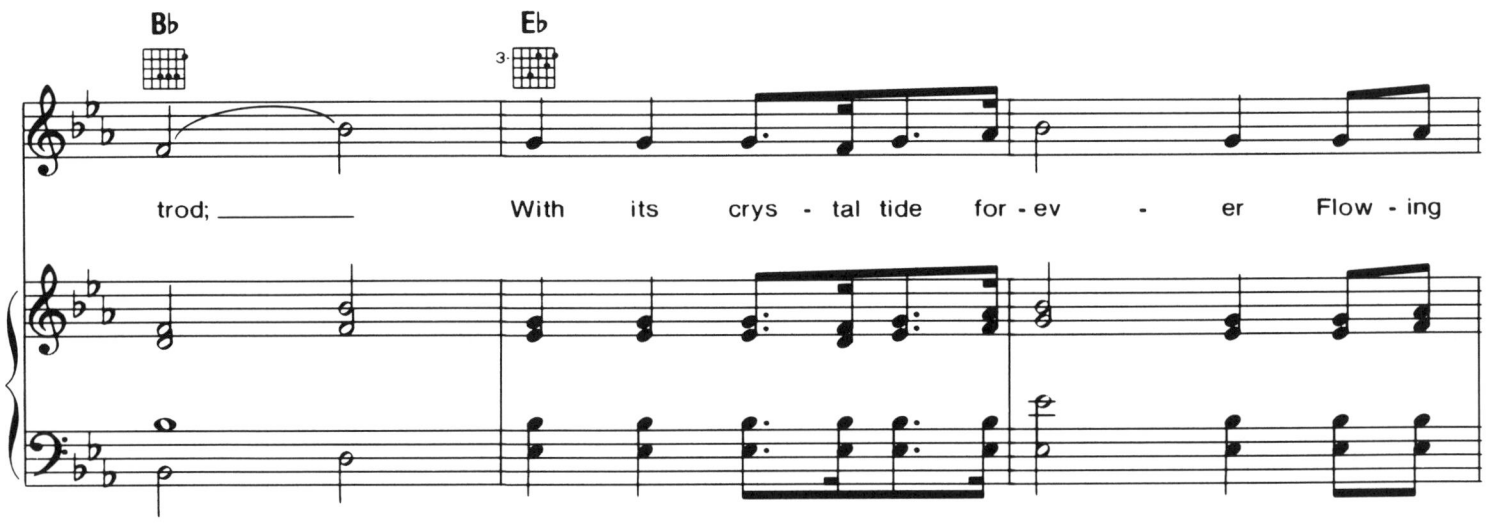
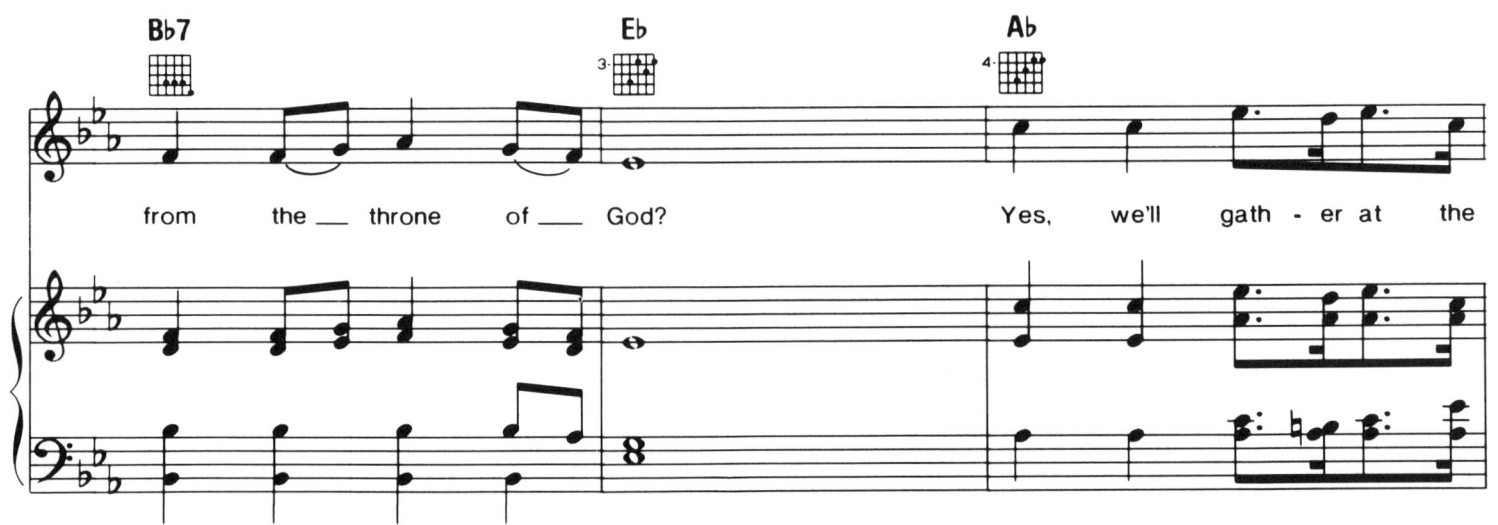

Copyright © 1983 by HAL LEONARD CORPORATION
International Copyright Secured   All Rights Reserved

2. On the margin of the river,
   Washing up its silver spray,
   We shall walk and worship ever
   All the happy, golden day.

3. On the bosom of the river,
   Where the Saviour King we own,
   We shall meet and sorrow never
   'Neath the glory of the throne.

4. Ere we reach the shining river,
   Lay we ev'ry burden down:
   Grace our spirits will deliver,
   And provide a robe and crown.

5. Soon we'll reach the shining river,
   Soon our pilgrimage will cease;
   Soon our happy hearts will quiver
   With the melody of peace.

Additional Verses

3. There's a light in the valley of death now for me,
   Since Jesus came into my heart!
   And the gates of the city beyond I can see,
   Since Jesus came into my heart!
   Refrain

4. I shall go there to dwell in that city, I know,
   Since Jesus came into my heart!
   And I'm happy, so happy, as onward I go,
   Since Jesus came into my heart!
   Refrain

Soon and Very Soon

Words and Music by
ANDRAÉ CROUCH

© 1976 BUD JOHN SONGS, INC. and CROUCH MUSIC
Admin. by EMI CHRISTIAN MUSIC PUBLISHING
All Rights Reserved   Used by Permission

Stepping on the Clouds

Words and Music by
LINDA STALLS

Moderately, in 2

One of these days_____ I'm gon-na leave,_____ one of these
moon, the stars and the plan-ets,_____ I'm gon-na

days_____ I'm go-ing home;_____
walk_____ on the milk-y white way;_____

© 1974 Word Music, Inc.
All Rights Reserved Used by Permission

SWEET BEULAH LAND

Words and Music by
SQUIRE PARSONS

© 1979 Kingsmen Publishing Company (BMI) (admin. by Brentwood-Benson Music Publishing, Inc.)
All Rights Reserved   Used by Permission

SWEET, SWEET SPIRIT

By DORIS AKERS

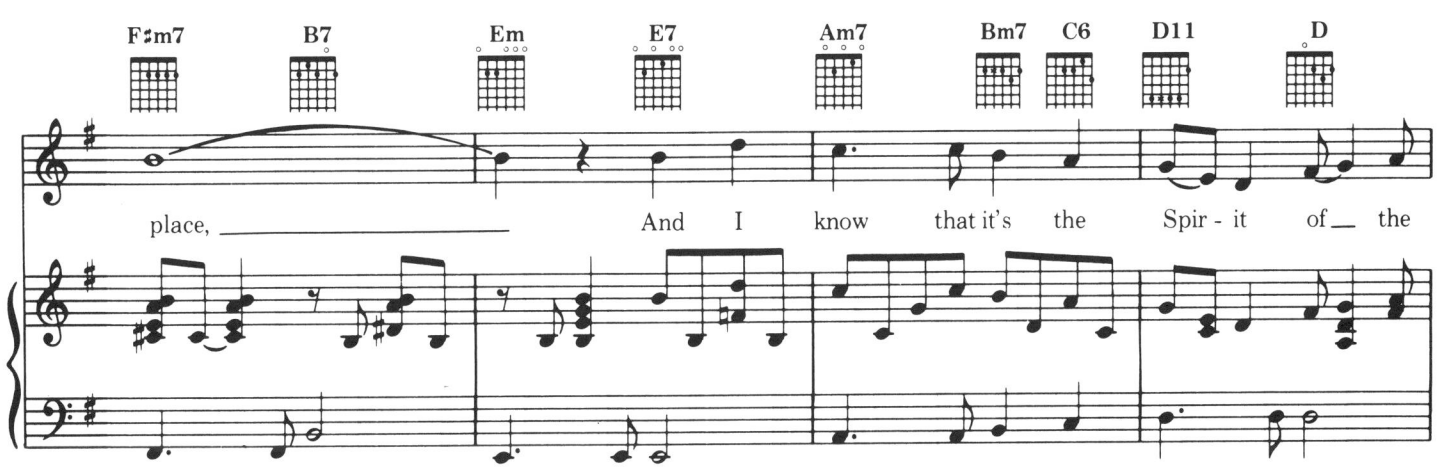

© Copyright 1962 (Renewed 1990) by MANNA MUSIC, INC., 35255 Brooten Road, Pacific City, OR 97135
All Rights Reserved   Used by Permission

SWEET BY AND BY

Words by SANFORD FILLMORE BENNETT
Music by JOSEPH P. WEBSTER

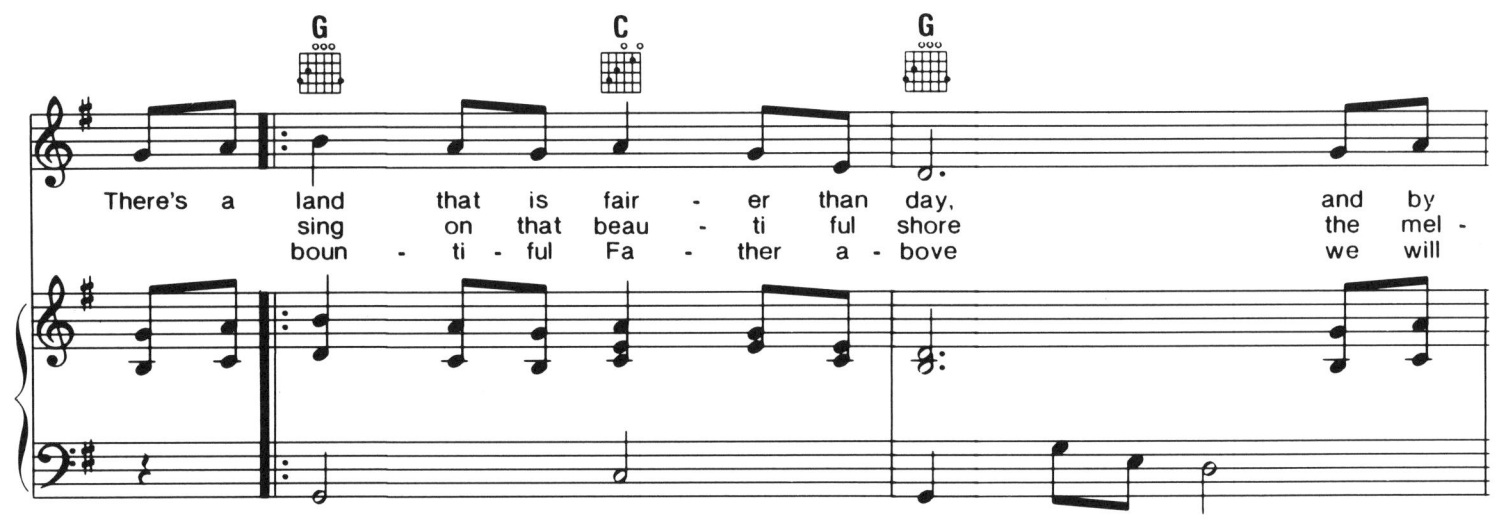

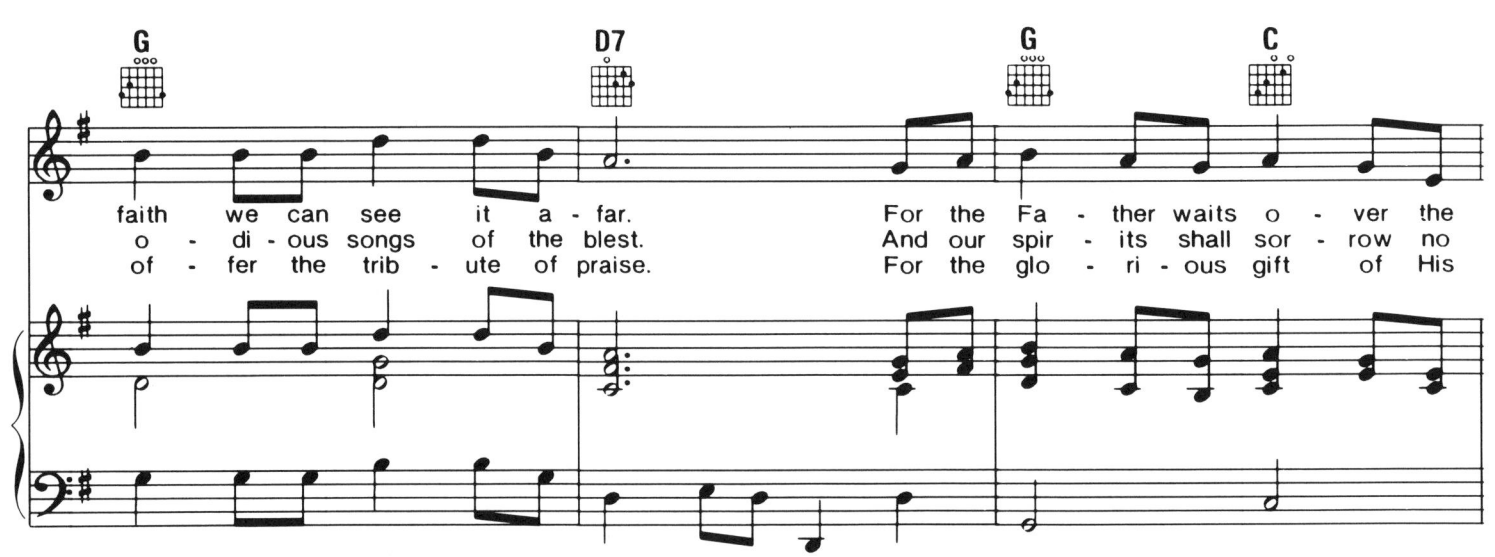

There's a land that is fair-er than day, and by faith we can see it a-far. For the Fa-ther waits o-ver the
sing on that beau-ti-ful shore the mel-o-di-ous songs of the blest. And our spir-its shall sor-row no
boun-ti-ful Fa-ther a-bove we will of-fer the trib-ute of praise. For the glo-ri-ous gift of His

Copyright © 1983 by HAL LEONARD CORPORATION
International Copyright Secured All Rights Reserved

Tears Are A Language God Understands

Words and Music by
GORDON JENSEN

Warmly

Of-ten you've won-dered why _____ tears come in-to your eyes, _____ and bur-dens seem to be much
left you low, _____ it caus-es tears to flow; things have not turned out the

more than you can stand. But God is
way that you had planned. But God won't for-

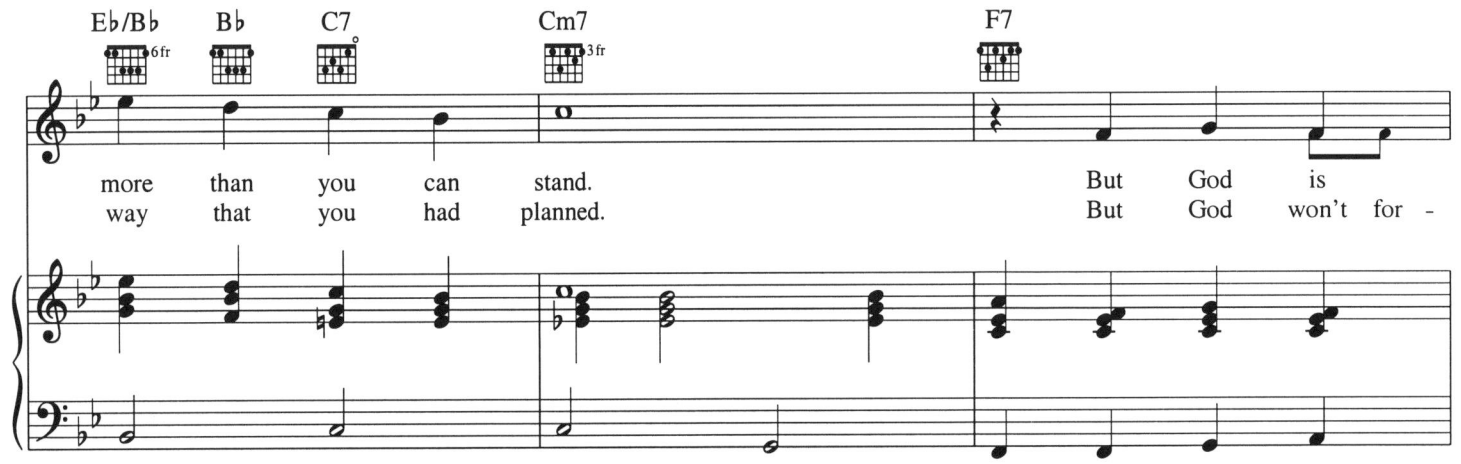

© 1971 New Spring Publishing, Inc. (ASCAP) (a div. of Brentwood-Benson Music Publishing, Inc.)
Copyright Renewed
All Rights Reserved   Used by Permission

THERE'S SOMETHING ABOUT THAT NAME

Words by WILLIAM J. and GLORIA GAITHER
Music by WILLIAM J. GAITHER

RECITATION

1. Jesus, the mere mention of His Name can calm the storm, heal the broken, raise the dead. At the Name of Jesus, I've seen sin-hardened men melted, derelicts transformed, the lights of hope put back into the eyes of a hopeless child...

   At the Name of Jesus, hatred and bitterness turned to love and forgiveness, arguments cease.

   I've heard a mother softly breathe His Name at the bedside of a child delirious from fever, and I've watched that little body grow quiet and the fevered brow cool.

   I've sat beside a dying saint, her body racked with pain, who in those final fleeting seconds summoned her last ounce of ebbing strength to whisper earth's sweetest Name - Jesus, Jesus...

2. Emperors have tried to destroy it; philosophies have tried to stamp it out. Tyrants have tried to wash it from the face of the earth with the very blood of those who claimed it. Yet still it stands.

   And there shall be that final day when every voice that has ever uttered a sound - every voice of Adam's race shall raise in one great mighty chorus to proclaim the Name of Jesus - for in that day "Every knee shall bow and every tongue shall confess that Jesus Chirst is Lord!!!"

   Ah - so you see - it was not mere chance that caused the angel one night long ago to say to a virgin maiden, "His Name shall be called Jesus." Jesus - Jesus - Jesus. You know, there is something about that Name...

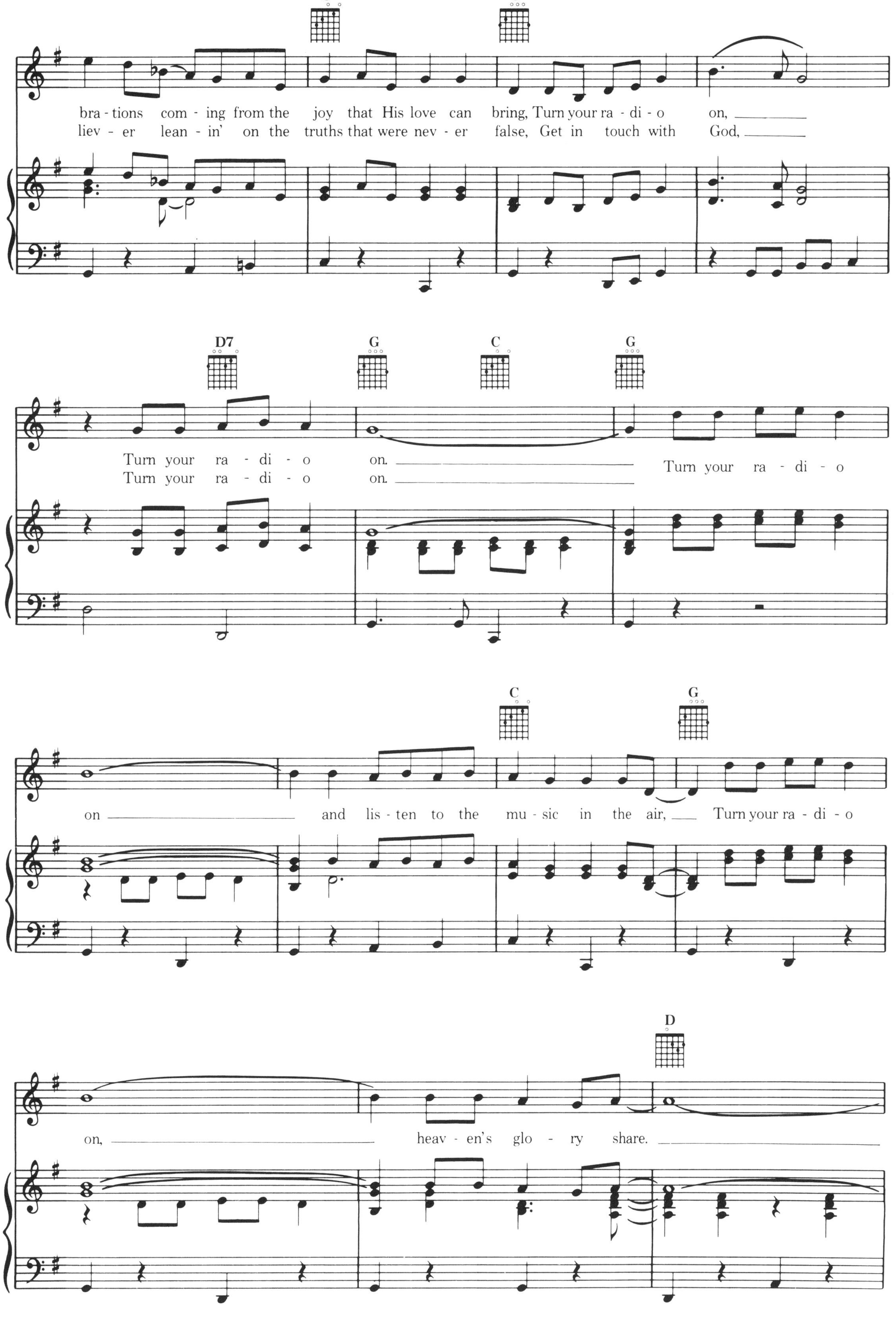
C
G
bra - tions com - ing from the joy that His love can bring, Turn your ra - di - o on,
liev - er lean - in' on the truths that were nev - er false, Get in touch with God,
D7
G
C
G
Turn your ra - di - o on.
Turn your ra - di - o on.
Turn your ra - di - o
C
G
on and lis - ten to the mu - sic in the air, Turn your ra - di - o
D
on, heav - en's glo - ry share.

THE UNCLOUDED DAY

Words and Music by
J.K. ALWOOD

UPON THIS ROCK

Words by GLORIA GAITHER
Music by DONY McGUIRE

© 1982, 1983 BUD JOHN SONGS, INC., IT'S-N-ME MUSIC and GAITHER MUSIC COMPANY
BUD JOHN SONGS, INC. and IT'S-N-ME MUSIC Admin. by EMI CHRISTIAN MUSIC PUBLISHING
All Rights Reserved   Used by Permission

WAYFARING STRANGER

Southern American Folk Hymn

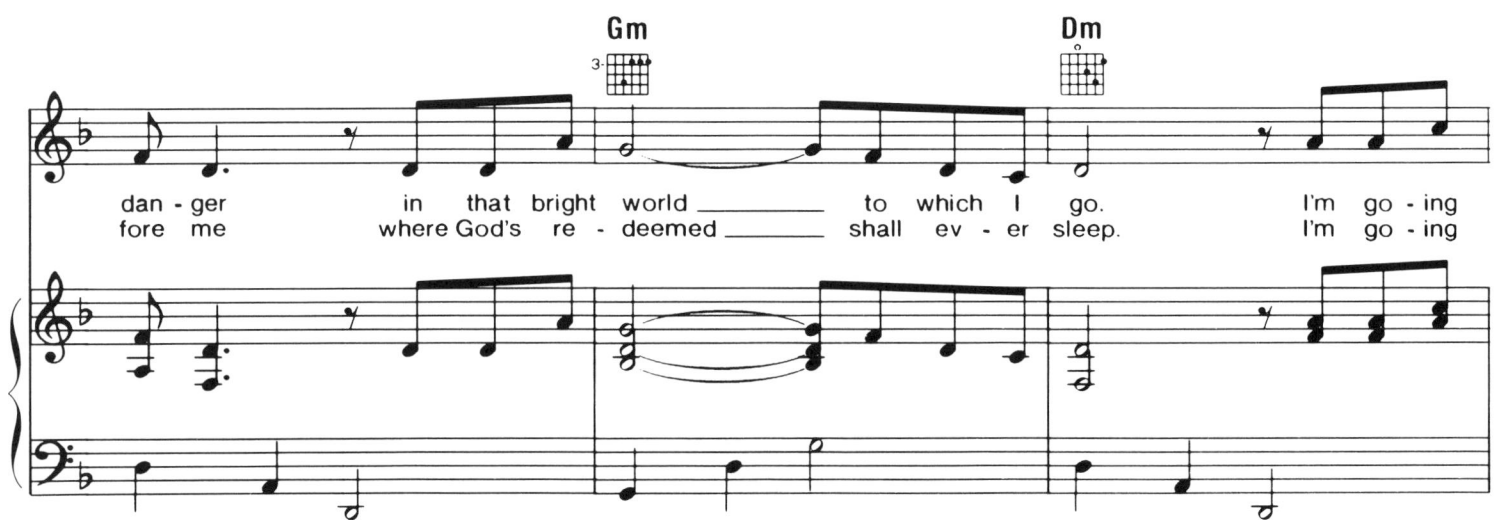

Copyright © 1983 by HAL LEONARD CORPORATION
International Copyright Secured All Rights Reserved

WE ARE SO BLESSED

Words and Music by GREG NELSON,
GLORIA and WILLIAM J. GAITHER

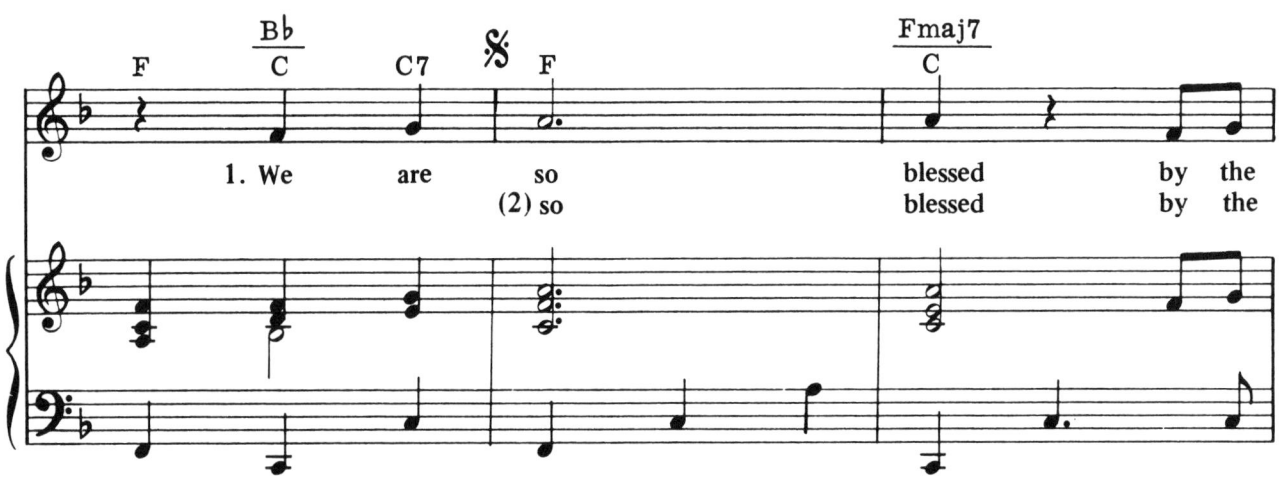

1. We are so blessed by the
(2) so blessed by the

gifts from Your hand, We just can't under-
things You have done, The vict'ries You've

© 1982 RIVER OAKS MUSIC COMPANY and GAITHER MUSIC COMPANY
All Rights for RIVER OAKS MUSIC COMPANY Admin. by EMI CHRISTIAN MUSIC PUBLISHING
All Rights for GAITHER MUSIC COMPANY Controlled by GAITHER COPYRIGHT MANAGEMENT
All Rights Reserved   Used by Permission

WE SHALL BEHOLD HIM

Words and Music by
DOTTIE RAMBO

Majestically

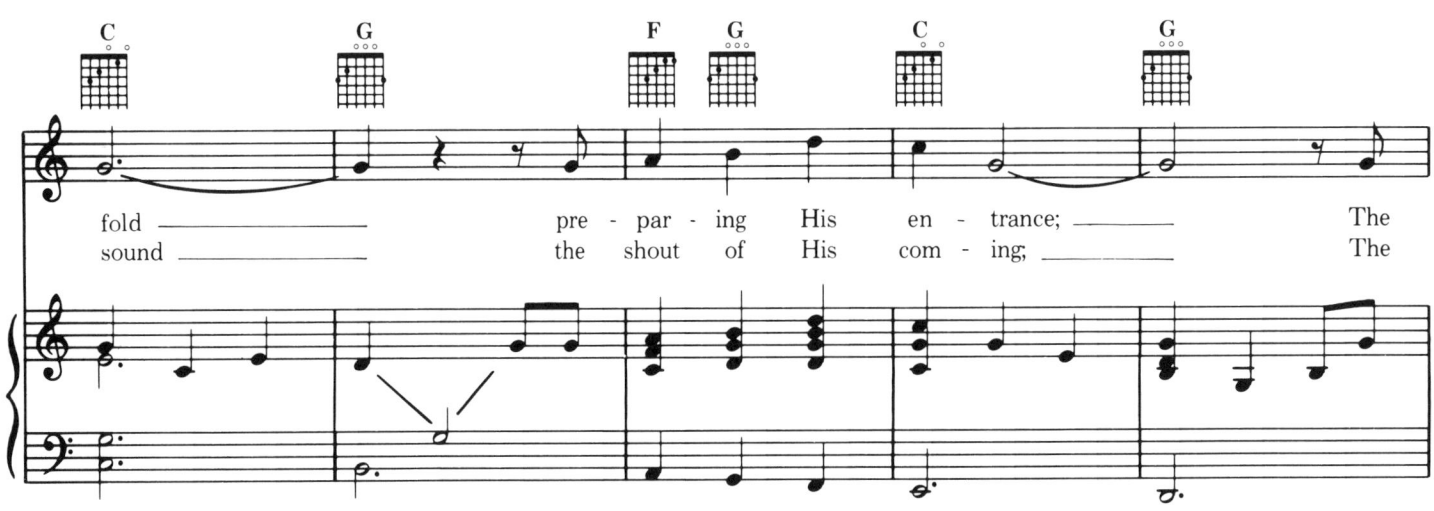

fold _____ pre - par - ing His en - trance; _____ The
sound _____ the shout of His com - ing; _____ The

stars will ap - plaud _____ Him _____ with thun - ders of
sleep - ing will rise _____ from their slum - ber - ing

© 1980 John T. Benson Publishing Co. (ASCAP) (admin. by Brentwood-Benson Music Publishing, Inc.)
All Rights Reserved   Used by Permission

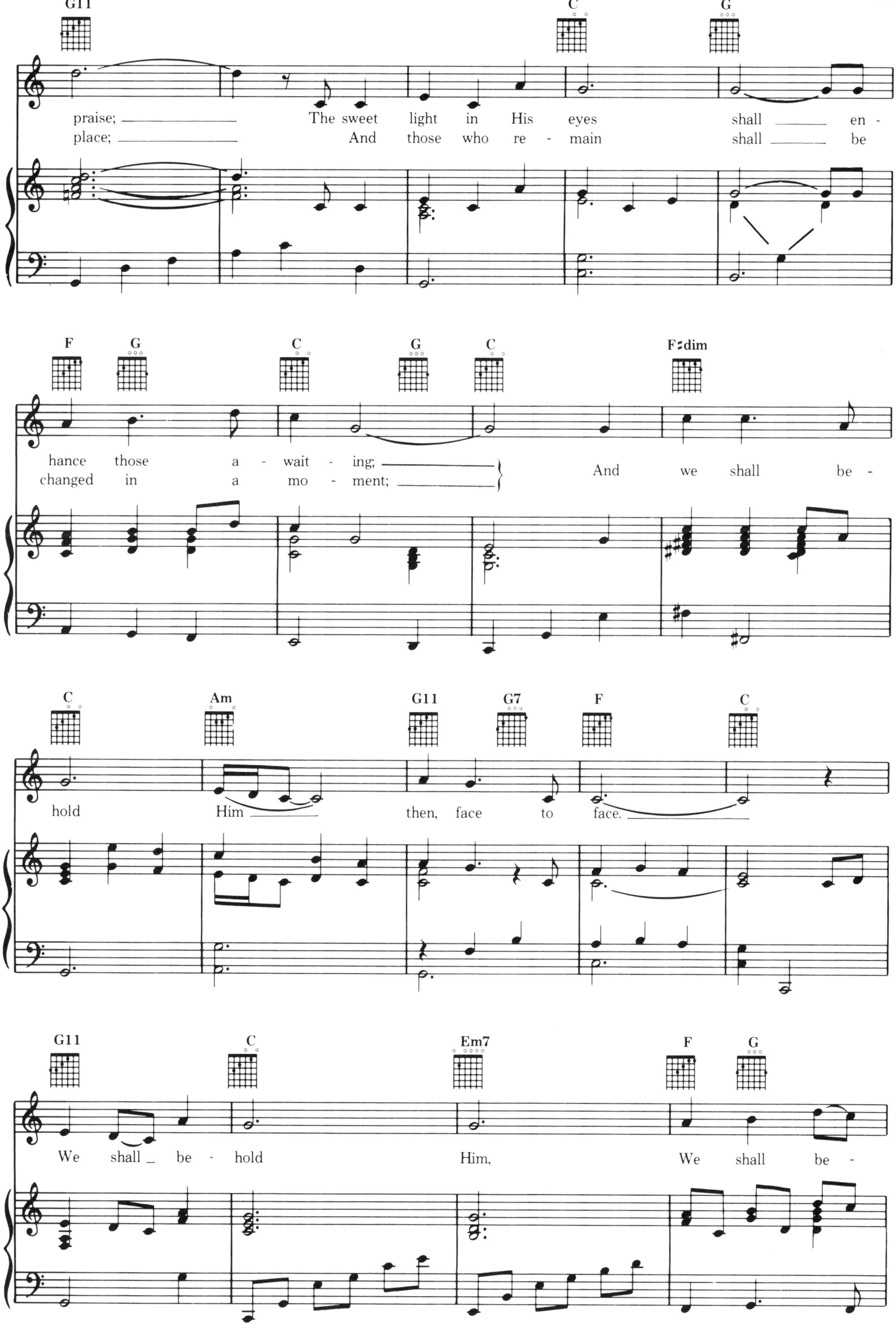
G11 C G
praise; The sweet light in His eyes shall en-
place; And those who re-main shall be
F G C G C F♯dim
hance those a-wait-ing;
changed in a mo-ment;
And we shall be-
C Am G11 G7 F C
hold Him then, face to face.
G11 C Em7 F G
We shall be-hold Him, We shall be-

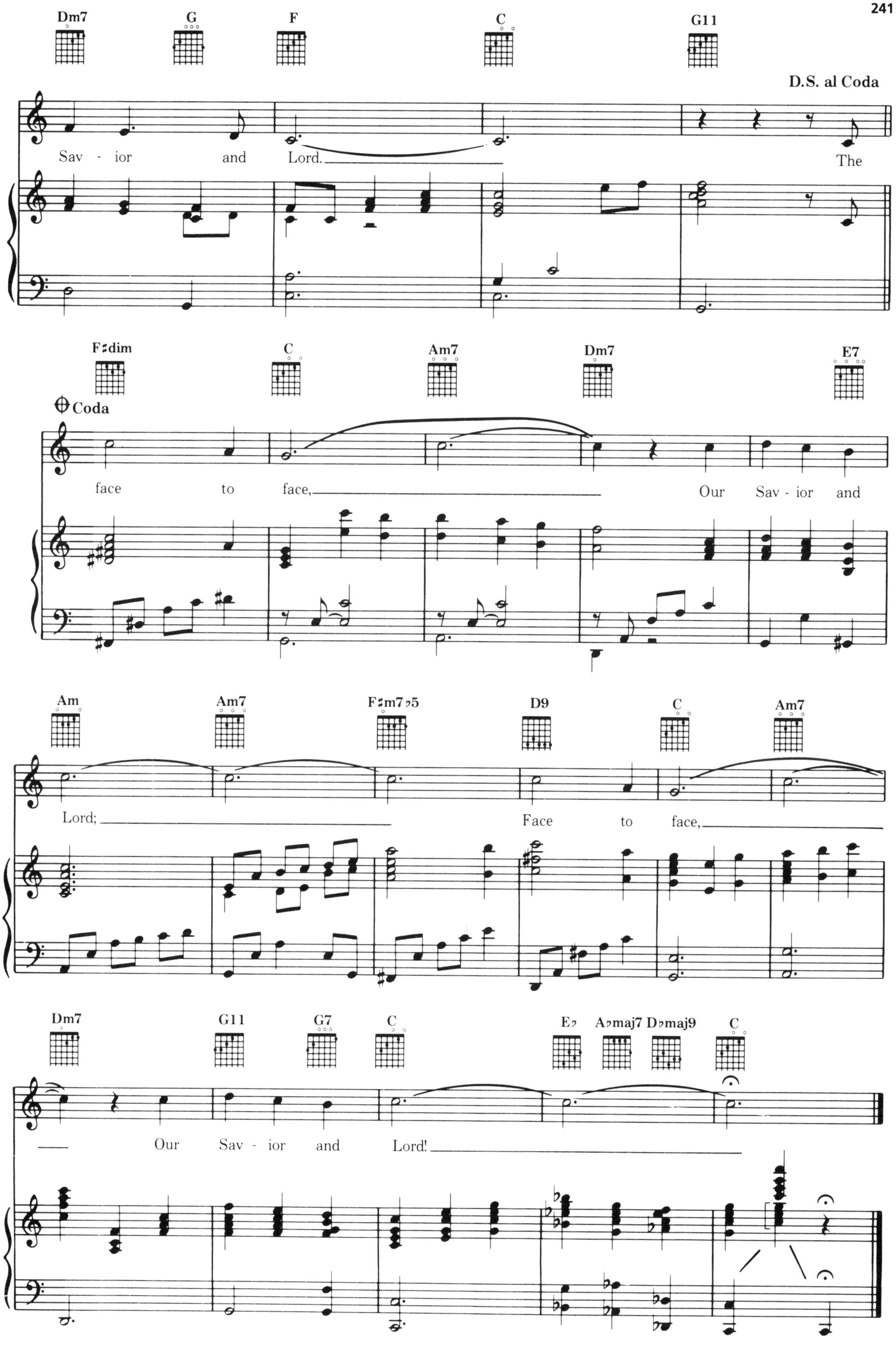
Dm7
G
F
C
G11
D.S. al Coda
Sav - ior and Lord. The
F♯dim
C
Am7
Dm7
E7
Coda
face to face, Our Sav - ior and
Am
Am7
F♯m7♭5
D9
C
Am7
Lord; Face to face,
Dm7
G11
G7
C
E♭
A♭maj7
D♭maj9
C
Our Sav - ior and Lord!

WE'LL UNDERSTAND IT BETTER BY AND BY

Words and Music by
CHARLES A. TINDLEY

Additional Verses

2. We are often destitute of the things that life demands,
   Want of food and want of shelter, thirsty hills and barren lands,
   We are trusting in the Lord, and according to His word,
   We will understand it better by and by.
   Refrain

3. Trials dark on every hand, and we cannot understand,
   All the ways that God would lead us to that blessed Promised Land;
   But He guides us with His eye and we'll follow till we die,
   For we'll understand it better by and by.
   Refrain

4. Temptations, hidden snares often take us unawares,
   And our hearts are made to bleed for a thoughtless word or deed,
   And we wonder why the test when we try to do our best,
   But we'll understand it better by and by.
   Refrain

WHEN THE ROLL IS CALLED UP YONDER

Words and Music by
JAMES M. BLACK

WILL THE CIRCLE BE UNBROKEN

Words by ADA R. HABERSHON
Music by CHARLES H. GABRIEL

Additional Verses

2. While we walk the pilgrim pathway,
   Clouds will overspread the sky;
   But when trav'ling days are over,
   Not a shadow, not a sigh!
   Refrain

3. Let us then be true and faithful,
   Trusting, serving ev'ryday.
   Just one glimpse of Him in glory
   Will the toils of life repay.
   Refrain

4. Onward to the prize before us!
   Soon His beauty we'll behold.
   Soon the pearly gates will open;
   We shall tread the streets of gold.
   Refrain

WHY ME?
(Why Me, Lord?)

Words and Music by
KRIS KRISTOFFERSON

Moderately, with a Gospel feeling

Why me, Lord? What have I ever done to deserve even
one of the pleasures I've known? Tell me, Lord, What did I ever
do that was worth loving you, Or the kindness you've shown?

If you think there's a way I can try to re-
pay all I've taken from you, May-be, Lord, I can show some-one
else what I've been thru my-self, On my way back to you.

© 1972 (Renewed 2000) RESACA MUSIC PUBLISHING CO.
All Rights Controlled and Administered by EMI BLACKWOOD MUSIC INC.
All Rights Reserved   International Copyright Secured   Used by Permission

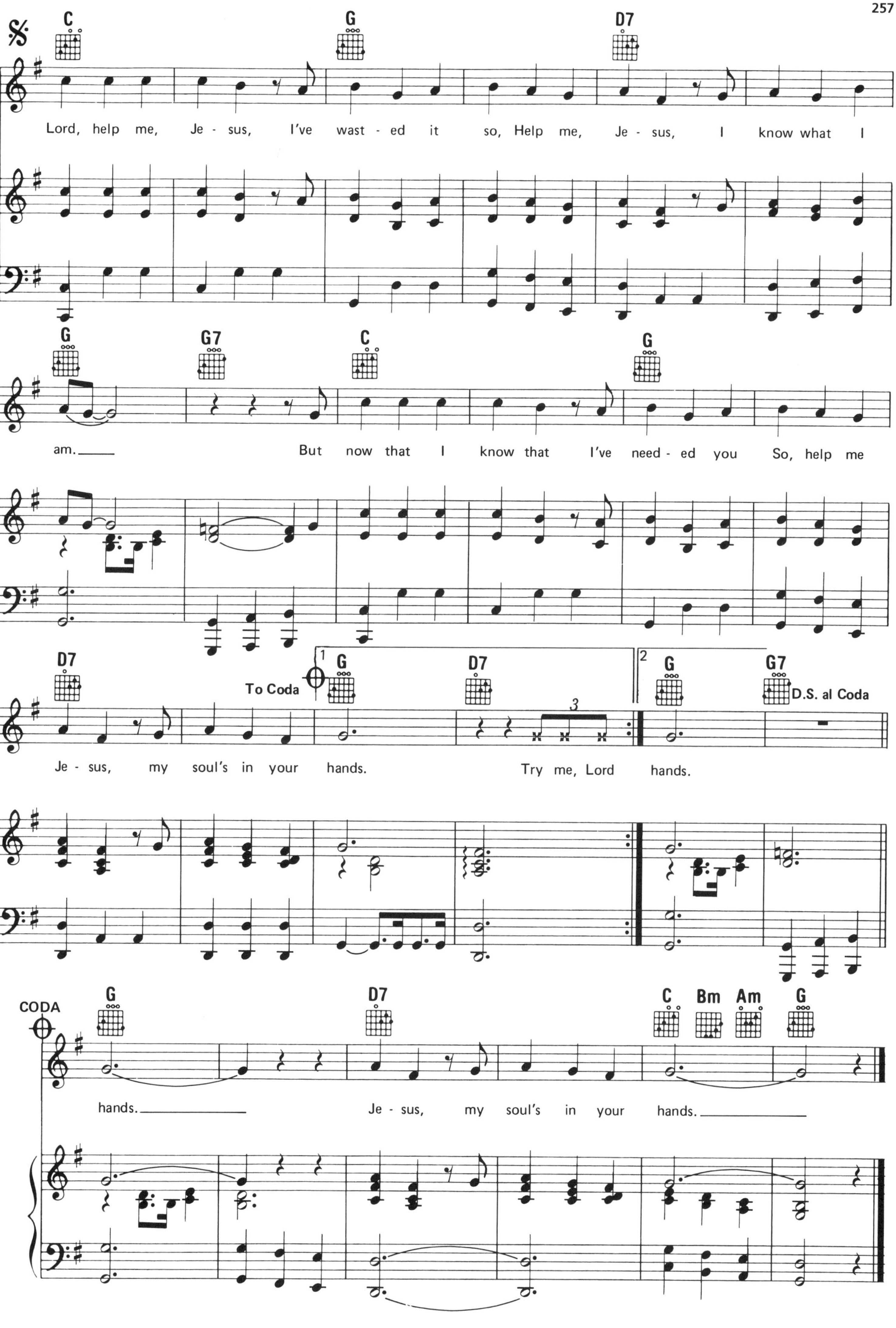
C G D7
Lord, help me, Je - sus, I've wast - ed it so, Help me, Je - sus, I know what I
G G7 C G
am. But now that I know that I've need - ed you So, help me
D7 To Coda 1 G D7 2 G G7 D.S. al Coda
Je - sus, my soul's in your hands. Try me, Lord hands.
CODA
G D7 C Bm Am G
hands. Je - sus, my soul's in your hands.

WINGS OF A DOVE

Words and Music by
BOB FERGUSON

Copyright © 1959 by Husky Music, Inc. and Larrick Music
Copyright Renewed
All Rights for the U.S. and Canada Administered by Unichappell Music Inc.
International Copyright Secured   All Rights Reserved

3. When Jesus went down to the waters that day,
   He was baptized in the usual way.
   When it was done, God blessed His Son.
   He sent him His love On the wings of a dove.

WITHOUT HIM

Words and Music by
MYLON R. LeFEVRE

Slowly

With - out Him I could do noth - ing, _____ With -
out Him I would be dy - ing, _____ With -

out Him I'd sure - ly fail; _____ With -
out Him I'd be en - slaved; _____ With -

out Him I would be drift - ing _____ Like a ship with -
out Him life would be hope - less _____ But with Je - sus, thank

Copyright 1963 (Renewed) Lefevre-Sing Publishing (BMI)
All Rights Controlled by Gaither Copyright Management
All Rights Reserved   Used by Permission

WRITTEN IN RED

Words and Music by
GORDON JENSEN

Big Books of Music

Our "Big Books" feature big selections of popular titles under one cover, perfect for performing musicians, music aficionados or the serious hobbyist. All books are arranged for piano, voice, and guitar, and feature stay-open binding, so the books lie flat without breaking the spine.

BIG BOOK OF BALLADS
63 songs.
00310485 ....$19.95

BIG BOOK OF BIG BAND HITS
84 songs.
00310701 ....$19.95

BIG BOOK OF BROADWAY
76 songs.
00311658 ....$19.95

BIG BOOK OF CHILDREN'S SONGS
55 songs.
00359261 ....$12.95

GREAT BIG BOOK OF CHILDREN'S SONGS
76 songs.
00310002 ....$14.95

MIGHTY BIG BOOK OF CHILDREN'S SONGS
65 songs.
00310467 ....$14.95

REALLY BIG BOOK OF CHILDREN'S SONGS
63 songs.
00310372 ....$15.95

BIG BOOK OF CHRISTMAS SONGS
126 songs.
00311520 ....$19.95

BIG BOOK OF CLASSICAL MUSIC
100 songs.
00310508 ....$19.95

BIG BOOK OF CONTEMPORARY CHRISTIAN FAVORITES
50 songs.
00310021 ....$19.95

BIG BOOK OF COUNTRY MUSIC
64 songs.
00310188 ....$19.95

BIG BOOK OF EARLY ROCK N' ROLL
99 songs.
00310398 ....$19.95

BIG BOOK OF GOSPEL SONGS
100 songs.
00310604 ....$19.95

BIG BOOK OF HYMNS
125 hymns.
00310510 ....$17.95

BIG BOOK OF JAZZ
75 songs.
00311557 ....$19.95

BIG BOOK OF LATIN AMERICAN SONGS
89 songs.
00311562 ....$19.95

BIG BOOK OF LOVE AND WEDDING SONGS
80 songs.
00311567 ....$19.95

BIG BOOK OF MOVIE MUSIC
72 songs.
00311582 ....$19.95

BIG BOOK OF NOSTALGIA
158 songs.
00310004 ....$19.95

BIG BOOK OF RHYTHM & BLUES
67 songs.
00310169 ....$19.95

BIG BOOK OF ROCK
78 songs.
00311566 ....$19.95

BIG BOOK OF STANDARDS
86 songs.
00311667 ....$19.95

BIG BOOK OF SWING
84 songs.
00310359 ....$19.95

BIG BOOK OF TORCH SONGS
75 songs.
00310561 ....$19.95

BIG BOOK OF TV THEME SONGS
78 songs.
00310504 ....$19.95

FOR MORE INFORMATION, SEE YOUR LOCAL MUSIC DEALER, OR WRITE TO:

HAL•LEONARD® CORPORATION
7777 W. BLUEMOUND RD. P.O. BOX 13819 MILWAUKEE, WI 53213

Prices, contents, and availability subject to change without notice.

Visit **www.halleonard.com**
for our entire catalog and to view our complete songlists.

The Finest Inspirational Music
Songbooks arranged for piano, voice, and guitar.

40 SONGS FOR A BETTER WORLD
40 songs with a message, including: All You Need Is Love • Bless The Beasts And Children • Colors Of The Wind • Everything Is Beautiful • He Ain't Heavy...He's My Brother • I Am Your Child • Love Can Build A Bridge • What A Wonderful World • What The World Needs Now Is Love • You've Got A Friend • and more.
00310096......................$15.95

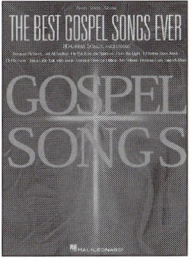
BEST GOSPEL SONGS EVER
80 of the best-loved Gospel songs of all time, including: Amazing Grace • At Calvary • Because He Lives • Behold the Lamb • Daddy Sang Bass • Get All Excited • His Eye Is on the Sparrow • I Saw the Light • I'd Rather Have Jesus • I'll Fly Away • Just a Little Talk With Jesus • Mansion Over the Hilltop • My Tribute • Precious Lord, Take My Hand • and more.
00310503......................$19.95

CHRISTIAN CHILDREN'S SONGBOOK
Over 80 songs from Sunday School, including: Awesome God • The B-I-B-L-E • The Bible Tells Me So • Clap Your Hands • Day by Day • He's Got the Whole World in His Hands • I Am a C-H-R-I-S-T-I-A-N • I'm in the Lord's Army • If You're Happy (And You Know It) • Jesus Loves Me • Kum Ba Yah • Let There Be Peace on Earth • This Little Light of Mine • When the Saints Go Marching In • and more.
00310472......................$19.95

CHRISTIAN WEDDING SONGBOOK
Over 30 contemporary Christian wedding favorites, including: Bonded Together • Butterfly Kisses • Commitment Song • Flesh of My Flesh • Go There with You • Household of Faith • How Beautiful • Love Will Be Our Home • Make Us One • Parent's Prayer (Let Go of Two) • This Is the Day (A Wedding Song) • and more.
00310681......................$16.95

CONTEMPORARY CHRISTIAN VOCAL GROUP FAVORITES
15 songs, including: The Basics Of Life • A Few Good Men • The Great Divide • Undivided • and more.
00310019......................$10.95

CONTEMPORARY CHRISTIAN WEDDING SONGBOOK
30 appropriate songs for weddings, including: Household Of Faith • Love In Any Language • Love Will Be Our Home • Parents' Prayer • This Is Love • Where There Is Love • and more.
00310022......................$14.95

COUNTRY/GOSPEL U.S.A.
50 songs written for piano/guitar/four-part vocal. Highlights: An American Trilogy • Daddy Sang Bass • He Set Me Free • I Saw The Light • I'll Meet You In The Morning • Kum Ba Yah • Mansion Over The Hilltop • Love Lifted Me • Turn Your Radio On • When The Saints Go Marching In • many more.
00240139......................$9.95

FAVORITE HYMNS
An outstanding collection of 71 all-time favorites, including: Abide With Me • Amazing Grace • Ave Maria • Bringing In The Sheaves • Christ The Lord Is Risen Today • Crown Him With Many Crowns • Faith Of Our Fathers • He's Got The Whole World In His Hands • In The Sweet By And By • Jesus Loves Me! • Just A Closer Walk With Thee • Kum Ba Yah • A Mighty Fortress Is Our God • Onward Christian Soldiers • Rock Of Ages • Swing Low, Sweet Chariot • Were You There? • and many more!
00490436......................$12.95

GREAT HYMNS TREASURY
A comprehensive collection of 70 favorites: Close To Thee • Footsteps Of Jesus • Amazing Grace • At The Cross • Blessed Assurance • Blest Be The Tie That Binds • Church In The Wildwood • The Church's One Foundation • God Of Our Fathers • His Eye Is On The Sparrow • How Firm A Foundation • I Love To Tell The Story • In The Garden • It Is Well With My Soul • Just A Closer Walk With Thee • Just As I Am • Nearer My God, To Thee • Now That We All Our God • The Old Rugged Cross • The Lily Of The Valley • We're Marching To Zion • Were You There? • What A Friend We Have In Jesus • When I Survey The Wondrous Cross • and more.
00310167......................$12.95

THE NEW YOUNG MESSIAH
Matching folio to the album featuring today's top contemporary Christian artists performing a modern rendition of Handel's *Messiah*. Features Sandi Patty, Steven Curtis Chapman, Larnelle Harris, and others.
00310006......................$16.95

OUR GOD REIGNS
A collection of over 70 songs of praise and worship, including: El Shaddai • Find Us Faithful • His Eyes • Holy Ground • How Majestic Is Your Name • Proclaim The Glory Of The Lord • Sing Your Praise To The Lord • Thy Word • and more.
00311695......................$17.95

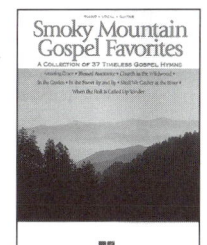
SMOKY MOUNTAIN GOSPEL FAVORITES
37 favorites, including: Amazing Grace • At Calvary • At The Cross • Blessed Assurance • Church In The Wildwood • I Love To Tell The Story • In The Garden • In The Sweet By And By • The Old Rugged Cross • Rock Of Ages • Shall We Gather At The River • Softly And Tenderly • Tell It To Jesus • Wayfaring Stranger • We're Marching To Zion • What A Friend We Have In Jesus • When The Roll Is Called Up Yonder • When We All Get to Heaven • and more.
00310161......................$8.95

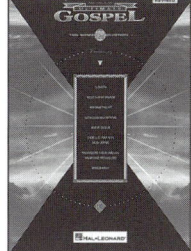
ULTIMATE GOSPEL – 100 SONGS OF DEVOTION
Includes: El Shaddai • His Eye Is On The Sparrow • How Great Thou Art • Just A Closer Walk With Thee • Lead Me, Guide Me • (There'll Be) Peace In The Valley (For Me) • Precious Lord, Take My Hand • Wings Of A Dove • more.
00241009......................$19.95

For more information, see your local music dealer, or write to:

7777 W. Bluemound Rd. P.O. Box 13819 Milwaukee, WI 53213

Visit us at www.halleonard.com for a complete listing of titles.

Prices, contents, and availability subject to change without notice.
Some products may not be available outside the U.S.A.